P9-EMQ-423

NOBODY LIKES YOU

MARC SPITZ

NOBODY LIKES YOU

INSIDE THE TURBULENT LIFE, TIMES, AND MUSIC OF GREEN DAY

HYPERION NEW YORK

Library of Congress Cataloging-in-Publication Data

Spitz, Marc.
   Nobody likes you : inside the turbulent life, times, and
music of Green Day / by Marc Spitz.—1st ed.
    p. cm.
   Includes bibliographical references and discography (p.)
   ISBN 1-4013-0274-2
   1. Green Day (Musical group) 2. Rock musicians—
United States—Biography. 3. Punk rock musicians—
United States—Biography. I. Title.
ML421.G74S65 2006
782.42166092'2—dc22
[B]   2006046248

Hyperion books are available for special promotions and pre-
miums. For details contact Michael Rentas, Assistant Director,
Inventory Operations, Hyperion, 77 West 66th Street, 12th
floor, New York, New York 10023, or call 212-456-0133.

Design by Fritz Metsch
Frontispiece photograph © Michael Muller/Corbis Outline

FIRST EDITION

10 9 8 7 6 5 4 3 2 1

For suburban punks everywhere

CONTENTS

MEET THE NEW PUNKS . . .

Giants Stadium, East Rutherford, New Jersey; very few rock 'n' roll bands are able to fill it. The Rolling Stones, David Bowie, U2, Dave Matthews Band, and local heroes Bon Jovi and, of course, Bruce Springsteen have all pulled it off at one point in their careers. Sometimes the football team that plays home games here can't bring in the 78,000 fans it takes to sell out this massive, cavernous building. Inside the big bowl, it seemed like a guitar chord had to travel several hundred yards across the field before the back row could tell it had been strummed. Giants Stadium was not a place for the self-conscious.

It was shortly before 9:00 p.m. on September 1, 2005, and emo-core group Jimmy Eat World had just walked off a stage the size of three small punk club spaces placed end to end. It was almost time for "Bunny" to do whatever it was "Bunny" did each night.

Dressed in a black long-sleeve shirt and red tie just as every other crew member, Bill Schneider, the coordinator of this massive production and a burly man with a vaguely Elvis-like hairdo, stalked through the concrete-wall dressing rooms to make sure every member of his team was aware of the time. Some of them nibbled at the cheese, crackers, and fruit that had been placed on the tables. Others gazed at the television screen. The *Best in Show* DVD flickered away as it had the previous night. This was a backstage area full of small rituals. Comfort and intensity coexisted surprisingly well.

"Thirty minutes!"

The bass player, Mike, usually coiled and hyper, was ill with the flu and seemed grayish and drawn. He lifted himself off the couch and padded down in his sneakers to the exercise room to suffer through a few miles on the stationary bicycle.

The lead singer, Billie Joe, compact, with a thick head of dyed black hair, fiddled with the arm bands on each of his sleeves. One read RAGE. The other read LOVE. He put on his shoes and walked over to the mirror to apply his kohl black eyeliner in lines thick enough to be picked up on the Diamond Vision screen. Close up, he looked fey. Later, from the back rows, while invoking the spirit of a street tough named St. Jimmy, he'll seem possessed.

"Fifteen minutes!"

The drummer, Tre, strong-chinned and jerky, bounded into the practice space and began emulating three-decade-old Keith Moon drum fills he'd clearly memorized.

"Ten minutes."

The singer, drummer, bass player, second guitarist, and horn and keyboard players gathered by the dressing room door and ran through harmonies for two of the most vocally complicated numbers in that night's set. The singer played guitar as they warmed up.

"Bunny!"

The door to the stage opened. A scream, like a Boeing jet engine, was heard as the beloved cheese-disco hit "YMCA" by the Village People pumped out of the stadium's massive speakers. Then, an intoxicated pink bunny rabbit staggered across the giant stage and clutched its plush and aching head in mock hangover agony while attempting to lead the masses in the song's spelling dance. (Bunny is actually a crew member, and sometimes Bunny really *is* hungover.)

At 9:25 p.m., "Blitzkrieg Bop" by the Ramones was pumped out over the field. It was always the last song to play on the mix CD that traveled with the band from city to city. (Small rituals.) When the Ramones's track faded, the lights went out and another solid, wall-like wave of painful white noise rolled around inside the hollow venue. "Also Sprach Zarathustra," composer Richard Strauss's piece of crescendo-building classical gas, played on the crowd's communal suspense. In the twentieth century, the composition had become a sort of sound track for pomposity (Stanley Kubrick's *2001: A Space Odyssey*), disco smarm (it was a big hit for Brazilian instrumentalist Deodato), and the bloat of Fat Elvis's white jumpsuit years. In the twenty-first, it functioned as an ironic but affectionate nod to such things. The band about to take the stage knew this well. In some ways, the members were as shocked as anyone that they had made it into that elite group with Mick, Keith, Bono, and . . . Dave. After all, they were supposed to be outsiders by nature and by the code of ethics they'd adhered to and had also been haunted by since their teens: punk rock. In other ways, this was where the secretly ambitous and competitive trio, with their unabashed love for pop music, meant to go. These had always been the two opposing sides of Green Day. In the early nineties, their ambitious and pop-loving side inspired them to leave their cozy but limited independent label; sign with a major one; record an album's worth of radio-ready, three-minute-long, irresistible, and oddly family-friendly music; and show the world what most of their peers in the indie scene already knew: Punk was some catchy stuff. Although they received a beating then at the hands of fundamentalists, Green Day never compromised their sound; they merely favored one side of it. Whenever they tired of being labeled as sellouts, balladeers, or cartoon pinups, they'd favor the other side (as they did with their second major label release, a menacing and frequently ugly bit of punker-than-you music that could stand combat boot to combat boot with any struggling, young, van-touring outfit's best). This duality was mirrored in the band's domestic life as well. Sometimes they were larger-than-life public figures: performers, businessmen, and spokesmen. Other times they were boyfriends, husbands, and dads, faced with home improvements and diaper-changing duties (which is about as *real* as you get).

The practicality they embraced in these moments was anti-star to the core. Interviews with major rock magazines were frequently scheduled in hotel suites simply so their children would get a chance to swim in the pool for a few hours. The members would show up for photo shoots wearing their own T-shirts, Dickies trousers, and sneakers, and any visual artiste or eager stylist who attempted to point them toward a rolling rack of costumes was met with a firm "No," a working-class sneer, and sometimes a finger to the chest.

Throughout the late nineties such constant personality swapping hobbled the band professionally and creatively. It destroyed a few families as well: Mike is divorced, and Tre is twice divorced. By the end of the decade, Green Day seemed less agile, like veteran athletes who trained only when necessary. In photos, they appeared apathetic, puffy, and weary.

A little more than two years ago, it would not have been shocking to see Green Day at the midpoint of a summer festival bill, slotted under bands almost half their ages—and playing the old hits because they had nothing new that could match them. They could have toured the House of Blues and shed circuit for the rest of their careers, making enough of a living to pay their bills. It wouldn't have been a glorious end for Green Day, who were once so genuinely exciting. As far as the rock 'n' roll cycle goes, it wouldn't have been an uncommon end either. Plenty of bands who've impacted the culture in one way or another now feel as if they've got nothing left to prove and are happy to collect their pop pensions well into middle age.

Where they arrived in 2004, however, *was* truly shocking. Their commercial and artistic resurgence was almost unprecedented in the pop world (Elvis Presley's '68 comeback television special, Bob Dylan's Grammy-winning *Time Out of Mind* stand among the exceedingly few return-to-form projects that, in many ways, actually improve on the old form). Personally this was a revolution too. Bands almost never rekindle an atmosphere of fun-seeking, brotherly affection after a decade plus of success (not without breaking up for a few years anyway, something Green Day never did). If anything, they grow even more fragmented. Somewhere in their third decade, Green Day had finally figured out what it meant to be Green Day. They'd become the biggest band in the world, outselling U2, Coldplay, and any other contender by finally allowing those two distinct halves, the compact-carrying Freddie Mercury–worshipper and the quasi-socialist punk pragmatist, to coexist without guilt or boundaries.

The resulting *American Idiot,* their eighth album, is revolutionary. It is a consistently brilliant and cohesive full-length album in an age of ninety-nine-cent digital singles. It presents an authentic political statement, but it also commands mass appeal despite the listener's voting proclivities because of the sheer inescapability of the song craft. *American Idiot* was a barrier-smashing masterpiece that not only raised the bar for punk rock, it gave the entire subculture (which had become a bit sluggish beneath the weight of its own inflexible musical template, eroding political commitment, and general mall-ification) a new vitality. The irony that Green Day, after all these years, was the band that accomplished this feat is not small.

Green Day has been subjected to cred-audits from the punker-than-thous ever since Billie Joe and Mike formed their first band, Sweet Children, in the late eighties. Even as they got set to blow away the Giants Stadium crowd at their biggest live show yet, there were fans who still would rather have seen them back on the streets—the Bowery, at Joey Ramone Place, specifically. That very week, CBGB, punk rock's Bethlehem, the un-cleanable bar where the Ramones, Blondie, Television Richard Hell, Talking Heads, and The Dead Boys got their starts, had finally lost its lease after a long battle with its landlord. A cultural landmark, but sadly, not an official one, CBGB in its original historic location had been condemned to die just a day before the Giants Stadium concert. (It finally closed in September 2006, but there are rumors that it will relocate, as all vital rock touchstones eventually do, to Las Vegas.) The following weeks saw circulating online and paper petitions. Editorials were written, and benefit concerts were staged. Public Enemy played, as did Institute, a negligible band fronted by former Bush lead singer Gavin Rossdale. Green Day did not play.

"Green Day was right across the river?" Kitty Kowalski, of the East Village punk band The Kowalskis, mused. She had attended the rallies the day before and was shaken by them. "Without CBGB, Green Day would not be selling out Giants Stadium, which holds one hundred CBGBs," Kowalski said.

Those who keep such sentiments often fail to acknowledge that punk rock really can survive only by staying relevant to young people. Nobody wants a quaint punk. The old guard were already on board. To appeal to a new generation, punk needs to change, mutate, remain exciting. And this, whether you like them or hate them, is exactly what Green Day have done. *American Idiot* was not only Green Day's second act, but also, in many ways, punk's. A great man named Sting once said, and I'm paraphrasing: "If you love punk, set it free." Green Day proved themselves true punks by finally letting go of it. They proved themselves rock stars by finally . . . letting it be (rockin').

Eight years ago, a reporter from the *Calagary Sun* asked Billie Joe Armstrong (lead singer, guitarist, and primary songwriter of the Bay Area trio) what punk rock was. Armstrong compared the act of describing punk rock with the act of "describing a smell." It is intangible, vague, haunting, and even maddening. When someone asked him the same question in 2004, he did not hesitate: "I don't question it anymore. It's me. It embodies me."

True enough, the guy had the word *punx* permanently carved into the flesh above his waist with a tattoo needle, but it wasn't until 2004 that he could finally and truly commit to it. "I've passed by Billie Joe a couple of times in our rock lives and can feel it in him," recalled Lenny Kaye, guitarist for another legendary CBGB-affiliated act called the Patti Smith Group. "He believes in the ideals that perhaps were passed along to him from a place like CBGB. They are continuing a tradition that perhaps has its roots there. That they're playing Giants Stadium is not important. That's just quantity. It makes a good end to the movie: When they're putting the padlock on the door of the club and then the camera pans up and you see Giants Stadium rocking. What's important is the fact that Green Day plays."

If the future of punk was ever in doubt, what with CBGB closing and bands such as Sum 41 existing, then all you had to do to be reassured was look at the wide grins on the faces of all those kids inside the stadium that night. Some of them were only eight or nine years old, brought to the concert by their parents. (Although he turned thirty-four in February of this year, Armstrong still graces the covers of the same teen magazines that he did at twenty-two. He is alone there, as far as his true peers go, representing for Generation X among the Chad Michael Murrays and Lindsay Lohans.) Many of these younguns had spiked hair and brand-new Green Day T-shirts from the merchandise stand. This new punk would mean everything to them, as the old punk meant everything to Mom and Dad.

One day, those T-shirts might be old and faded. And maybe Green Day will be living down the ghost of *American*

Idiot. Maybe they already are, only two years after Giants Stadium. But it doesn't matter. Because somewhere in the world, a band will be playing with the formula, taking what was invented with *American Idiot,* expanding it, and remaking punk rock's future yet again. It would be foolish, at this point, to rule out that the band may be Green Day themselves.

NOBODY LIKES YOU

Chapter One

TWIN JESUSES OF SUBURBIA

On October 13, 2005, Green Day performed one of their last U.S. dates on the thirteen-month-long, 130-date *American Idiot* tour. The "secret" show at San Francisco's Warfield Theater (a poorly kept secret, as most secrets are in the information age) was designed to be a triumphant finale and a thank-you to loyal local fans who could see a full Green Day concert at venues a fraction the size of the sports arenas they'd been playing all year. Makeup dates in the Midwest (and a short trip to Australia) prevented the band from fully unpacking, but the sold-out show succeeded as a genuine homecoming because the appropriate emotions were stirred.

Billie Joe Armstrong was reflective that night. Just a day earlier while onstage at the El Rey Theatre in Los Angeles he was pissed off as he and the band ran through *American Idiot* in its entirety for youngish Hollywood types such as *Garden State*'s Zack Braff and *Lost*'s Matthew Fox. Maybe his wistfulness was because the Warfield show, unlike the El Rey, was *not* being broadcast across the universe via America Online. More likely, however, it was because Armstrong may have realized that after selling millions of records and winning dozens of major music awards he'd finally really made it into the city.

"I grew up in a town called Rodeo," Armstrong said at the Warfield as a means to introduce the evening's second song. (The first song had been, as it had all year, "American Idiot.") "It's right off the 80 at Willow," he continued, identifying the actual exit. "And it was the inspiration for this next song. This is 'Jesus of Suburbia.'"

"Jesus of Suburbia," the second track on *American Idiot* and the first of the two suites that classify the album as the first punk rock opera, is Armstrong's most personal song and, to his mind, the high point of his career as a songwriter. "I think it's the one I'm proudest of," Armstrong told me in a 2005 interview in *Spin*. "I never get tired of playing it live. It always makes me emotional."

"Jesus of Suburbia" roils with that weird mix of boredom and anger that's almost an epidemic among suburban kids. These nameless, faceless millions are the sons (and daughters) of rage and love, as the song's opening line declares. They're special, each of them, in their own way, but it seems like nobody knows or cares. So they dream of running away to the city, where these qualities will finally be recognized and appreciated.

"It's that lost feeling," Armstrong explains. "Hanging out at the 7-Eleven. Disenfranchised. Alienated. You just get that feeling of 'I've got to get out of here. There's more to life than this town.'"

Rodeo has not changed much since the mid-eighties, when a fourteen-year-old Billie Joe Armstrong walked its streets at night, getting stoned and fantasizing about escape. If you really want to get an idea of what it must have been like to be so close to the city and yet, culturally, light years away, spend a few hours, maybe a half a day, in San Francisco before taking the thirteen-mile trip west on Interstate 80 (off at Willow).

San Francisco is a European-style city where serene beauty and seedy danger are often separated only by a few paces in either one direction or another. As a result, it's an urban environment that compels you to be alert and engaged. The only source of true peril in Rodeo may be breathing. "I went to elementary school [by the refineries]," Armstrong recalled in a 1995 interview in the punk 'zine *bUH*. "They used to send kids home all the time for headaches."

"You'd get a phone call and you'd have to lock all your doors and windows because something was coming out of the refineries that's not good for you [to breathe]," says Armstrong's older sister Anna Armstrong Humann (she still lives there, as do Billie Joe's mother and several close friends). "We're on the water and there's a lot of old architecture, but there's just no money that comes into [Rodeo]. It's unincorporated, so there's no government or any kind of organized group that tries to keep things going. We've been called the armpit of Contra Costa County."

Rodeo is seven and a half square miles and has a population of about 9,000 (compared with San Francisco's nearly 800,000 or even Oakland's 200,000). New Rodeo with its post-war tract houses is the posh section of town. Here, the average family income is about sixty thousand dollars a year. The strip that runs through it is a landscape study of mini-malls and the kinds of modernized gas stations/convenience stores you'd find in any suburb.

Once you cross over into Old Rodeo, however, you get the eerie feeling that things have not changed in decades. It's very much a small town with one Chinese restaurant, one liquor store, a taxidermist, a bait shop, and many ball fields (one road sign informs visitors they've entered "Baseball Town U.S.A."). There are no real yards to divide each small, stucco home. The sun seems to hang lower and heavier than anywhere else on the map, and you can taste chemicals in the air. Drive a little farther past the Carquinez Bridge and you will soon see why. In the distance, about a mile and a half from the fields where the kids play, is a vast block of towering stacks. Oil refineries that turn crude oil into gas and diesel fuel twenty-four hours a day shoot smoke into the air. "Refinery Row," the residents call it, and its proximity to the residential area may seem normal to them at this point, but it's shocking to people who visit from San Francisco (or anywhere really). "They have to refine oil somewhere," one reasons. They do it here.

"When we were young, and we'd be driving home from someplace, the refineries would be right there and we'd go, 'Oh, look at Disneyland,'" jokes Anna. "It was killing us, but we didn't think about it."

Armstrong, of course, got out of Rodeo—pronounced *row-day-o*, not like the bronco riding competitions for which the town was originally named. But there's still some Rodeo in him. "It's like I am those refineries," he once told the *San Francisco Chronicle*, "I *am* the suburbs."

•

Rodeo's size and limitations wouldn't matter for years, of course. Discounting the compromised oxygen, it was as fulfilling a place as any for a child to grow up.

Billie Joe Armstrong, born February 17, 1972, in Oakland, was by all accounts an adorable child.

"He was real cute," concurs his older brother David. "Long, curly hair. Girls loved him. My sister's girlfriends just adored him. Even as a kid he had a lot of charisma."

Billie Joe was the youngest of Andy and Ollie Armstrong's five children (in addition to David and Anna, there was older sisters Holly and Marci, and older brother Allen, who at twenty-two had already moved out of the house by the time Billie Joe was born).

Both parents came from remarkably large families, so the Armstrong brood didn't seem at all odd. "My mom is one of twelve kids," Anna says. "My father was one of eight. So there are a lot of aunts and uncles, and I think at this point twenty-three or twenty-four grandkids. Big family gatherings."

Ollie was a part-time waitress at local eateries like A Place at the Point in nearby Richmond and later Rod's Hickory Pit in addition to being a homemaker. She was already used to the work required to run such a substantial home. She arrived in California by train as a teenager in the late forties (by way of Sperry, Oklahoma) after her father (who arrived on horseback) settled and sent for her and her mother. By the time her youngest, with his cherubic face and mischievous smile full of crooked teeth, began walking and talking, she considered herself semiretired when it came to discipline. "My mom got less and less strict with each kid," Armstrong told the *Alternative Press*.

Andy, a bearish former boxer, was born and raised in Berkeley. He was an amateur jazz drummer, and met Ollie during one of his sporadic gigs. They shared a love of music and dancing. Like his soon-to-be bride, however, Andy knew what it was like to work hard with little relief. "My father had been driving trucks since the fifties. Cement trucks, any kind of truck," David remembers. Andy had found steady employment driving big rigs for the Safeway grocery chain, and when the family settled into a three-bedroom house in the Rodeo suburbs, after stints in Fairfield and Richmond, they were enjoying a more or less middle-class existence (the real estate cost around 70,000 dollars at the time, and remains to this day, the Armstrong family house).

Although Billie Joe and his brother David shared a pair of bunk beds, and Anna and her sisters shared their one bedroom (prompting not a few fights), life in Rodeo was comfortable for the close-knit Armstrongs. "I never remember us struggling for money," David says. "We always had what we wanted. My dad would have to go on an overnight every couple of weeks, but he was home mostly every night."

The family wasn't especially political, nor were they religious. "My dad was Catholic," Billie Joe says, "and my mom was, I don't know. Some kind of Christian. It was never really forced on us." Music, however, was a different story. While Andy had his modern jazz favorites, Ollie was a serious fan of classic country music like Hank Williams and Patsy Cline (as well as some modern classicists like Dolly Parton and Willie Nelson). Andy's drum kit had a permanent space in the family sitting room. "Unless my dad was playing a gig somewhere," David says, "then he'd take it apart and take it with him. But he'd always set it right back up when he was done. Me and Billie learned how to play drums early." Once they were old enough, the children were encouraged to structure some of that free-form expression.

Fiatarone's was, and still is, the local music shop, run by Marie Louise Fiatarone and her husband Jim. Jim Fiatarone (now deceased) was the first person outside the family to notice that Billie Joe Armstrong was special and the first ever to preserve it on vinyl.

"Billie Joe's mother brought him and [two of his sisters] in because she was signing them up for piano lessons," Marie Louise recalls. "Jim took one look at him and said, 'He looks like he really belongs in show business. Why don't you take him in the studio and see if he can sing.'" Marie Louise, always one to encourage young talent, asked Billie Joe if he would be interested in singing for her. The response was quick and affirmative, as if he'd been waiting to perform outside of the family living room. When Fiatarone sat Billie Joe down in the back room and lead him through some rudimentary standards, she was shocked by the results.

"We did 'He's Got the Whole World in His Hands,'" Fiatarone remembers. "And he could just move and change keys and sing right on pitch. This is very rare. It's rare for boys particularly because they don't listen as well as girls do."

David Armstrong remembers the formative event a little differently [Fiatarone might have politely blocked him out of her memory]. "We all went in that day." He laughs. "All us kids, and they put us all in the room together to sing. And I got pulled out. Billie was obviously the singer in the family. Right from day one. Mrs. Fiatarone took to him right away."

Ollie Armstrong was proud that her son's abilities were recognized by these professionals and happily signed Billie Joe up for singing lessons at Fiatarone's, as well as piano lessons, once a week. The cost might have been prohibitive had Mr. Fiatarone not suggested a way for the two families to help each other out. Fiatarone's was something of an indie record label as well, and Jim Fiatarone was its chief producer, songwriter, and distributor. He'd previously released a single called "Make My World Beautiful," a self-penned original, interpreted by a Japanese singing star named Yukiko.

"My husband thought it would be a great idea for this little guy to sing the new song that we wrote," Fiatarone says. "We took him to Fantasy Studios [in Berkeley]. And he just put the earphones on and we did it right there. My son Jim played guitar, and I played keyboards." (Armstrong obviously did not know it at the time, but he would record *Dookie* in that very building sixteen years later.)

Although nearly impossible to find (an eBay copy will set you back at least fifteen hundred dollars), Armstrong's "debut" single, a vinyl 45 with a print run of only 800 copies, was a pleasingly bouncy bit of sunshine pop called "Look for Love." Armstrong's adenoidal tone reminds the listener of the young Donnie Osmond: not exactly soulful but certainly dead on pitch. The B-side is a patient and sweet interview with the eager, and very young song stylist.

JIM FIATARONE: Billie Joe, you've just made your first record. How does it feel?
BILLIE JOE: Um . . . wonderful!

You can hear a sampling of the interview at the beginning of Green Day's 2001 *International Superhits!* CD. In the age of Fleetwood Mac and Elton John, "Look for Love" didn't change the pop landscape forever. It did, however, earn Armstrong his first bit of press: a 500-word item in the local newspaper, titled "Billie Joe Armstrong, 5, Might Be on His Way to the Top." A nifty partnership with the Fiatarones also ensued. Armstrong was entered into dozens of regional songwriting contests.

"I would do the background cassettes he'd use," Fiatarone recalls. "He'd sing a lot of Broadway show tunes. George M. Cohan. We did the theme to 'New York, New York' once."

Armstrong's knack for live performance inspired his father, and soon the pair were touring convalescent homes and Shriners Hospitals across Northern California, putting on monthly feel-good pageants for the elderly and infirm. Billie Joe sang, Andy Armstrong played drums, and the Fiatarones and their other students filled in on everything else. "I learned a lot about how to be onstage," Armstrong says. "[Since then] I've always looked at it like I'm a showman."

"The older ladies just absolutely loved him," Fiatarone confirms. "He'd go out and shake hands with them and talk to them. For a while, I think there was a little concern that this image doesn't go with his current image. But when you're five it's another story."

"He was like Shirley Temple," Anna says. "He definitely had a presence about him at that age, where he could go on-stage and sing and it wasn't cheesy. He came off very naturally and relaxed. It wasn't this idea of 'Let's have a famous kid' or anything. Like [Mouseketeer-era] Britney Spears or Justin Timberlake. It was more of a fun thing for him to do, working with our dad."

Billie Joe's parents purchased a cherry-red Hohner guitar for him when he was seven, and the near-prodigy proved as equally quick a study with it as he had been with his vocal scales and tones. The remainder of the seventies were idyllic years for the Armstrongs. The eighties would be difficult. Billie Joe's approach to music was passionate, but it also befit his youth and essentially happy-go-lucky air. He was a vessel, an entertainer. By late spring of 1982, however, he would begin to turn this energy inward in an effort to make sense of new and troubling emotions: confusion, anger, loss.

Andy Armstrong had always been physically strong. He was rarely sick, but he'd been feeling ill. After a trip to the doctor and a battery of tests, he was informed that he was suffering from esophageal cancer. The shock was extreme. The prognosis was poor. The family gathered around the kitchen table one night and Andy broke the news to them in a voice choked with sadness and fear. He was only fifty-one.

"We were all just shell-shocked," Anna says. "Our whole lives just ended at that point, and a new life started for us."

The reality of it all was almost inconceivable for the entire family but especially so for ten-year-old Billie Joe, who had been habitually sheltered by his parents and older siblings. This was something from which they could not protect him, and as Andy lost weight and strength, Billie Joe felt increasingly helpless. He couldn't make this go away with a song and a charming smile.

"My dad said on his deathbed, 'Make sure you take care of Billie Joe,'" David recalls. "'Cause he was the youngest. And the creative one. After that I became the bug catcher. Whenever there was a spider in the house, my sister or my mother would run to me." Indulging Billie simply because he was cute ceased as well. For a time, anyway, David assumed the role of strict (albeit still teenaged) disciplinarian. "I was hard on him," he admits, "but it was because I was worried about him. I thought I was his father."

Andy passed away on September 1, 1982, just four months after being diagnosed. During the funeral, Billie Joe broke down in tears.

"It changed him," Anna observes. "It touched him in a way that made him become different. When I think about Billie in that time, I have an image and that was at the actual funeral. We were at the cemetery and he kissed a flower and he laid it on my father's casket."

The family went about mourning in their own ways. Ollie

went from part- to full-time shifts at Rod's Hickory Pit. "The whole dynamic of the family changed," Anna says. "I think it was overwhelming for her. Her way of dealing with anything was, and is to this day, to work. To stay busy. And I think that kept her out of the house and allowed her to in some ways avoid what her children were going through. In a lot of ways, all of us kind of had to go through that grieving and mourning by ourselves. We didn't necessarily know how to be with each other during that time. We didn't know how to help each other, or support each other, because it was all just so foreign and strange."

Billie Joe dealt with Ollie's absence by assisting the family with laundry and dishwashing duties. He coped with the loss of his father by traveling deeper and deeper into the exploration of the one thing that made him feel strong and capable when so many situations around him now seemed foreign and frightening: music. By 1982, MTV, which had launched the previous year, was in thousands of California homes, including the Armstrongs'. Billie Joe would sit for hours in front of the television set with his brothers and sisters, trying to handicap which video would be selected next from the cable channel's then paltry library: Rod Stewart or Duran Duran? Pat Benatar or Loverboy? Music videos excited him, but the Beatles records his older brother Allen handed down around this time obsessed, inspired, and healed him. "It all sort of happened at the same time of my father dying," Anna says. "Not too many fifth-graders were writing songs. He really started exploring that part of himself, and creating his own music."

Local guitar teacher George Cole picked up where the Fiatarones left off when it came to focusing Billie Joe's raw ability without resorting to the kind of overbearing strictness that discourages many pupils from continuing their music studies. At first Billie Joe resisted learning music theory, and preferred to jam or play the Beatles songs that comforted him in his bunk bed. He could render these nearly exactly and by ear. To this day, they remain his favorite group, and their influence on Green Day, although not overt, is consistent and strong. Like the Fab Four, he held great reverence for classic pop-song structure. And also like John, Paul, George, and Ringo, he couldn't (and wouldn't) read a note. He didn't even know how to write out the new songs that were coming into his head. Songs that took these thick, indelible Lennon/McCartney (and sometimes John/Taupin) melodies and adapted them, slightly, into something new and exclusive. Fortunately Cole had an easy shorthand with his student, not to mention a patient air. When Billie Joe presented Cole with the new Van Halen album *Diver Down,* Cole taught him how to approximate already iconic guitarist Eddie Van Halen's hammer technique. Van Halen, with David Lee Roth's enviable swagger (if you're ten, anyway) and Eddie Van Halen's awe-inspiring technical proficiency, would prove to be another great influence. Unlikely, if you employ some hindsight, but Green Day's confidence in their musicianship and ability to make three-chord punk songs much, much bigger than they actually are, begins with Ed and Diamond Dave. Cole and Billie Joe would frequently spend afternoons jamming together, free-form style, with the teacher winging off as many odd notes as his pupil. Cole's guitar was a powderblue Fernandez Stratocaster (an expertly constructed copy of the famous—and much more expensive—Fender Stratocaster, played most famously by Jimi Hendrix).

Armstrong fetishized his teacher's guitar, partly because the blue instrument had a sound quality and Van Halen–worthy fluidity he couldn't get from his little red Hohner. He prized it mostly, however, because of his relationship with Cole, another father figure after the death of Andy. He let his obsession with the guitar, which he simply called "Blue," be known to his family. Noticing how happy and alive the lessons with Cole made the still-grieving boy feel, Ollie made arrangements to purchase "Blue" from Cole as an early Christmas gift.

"I don't know how my mom did it, but she got the money together and bought 'Blue' from George," David Armstrong recalls. "At that time we were struggling, and the three or four hundred dollars that it cost wasn't money she just had sitting around." Ollie's investment has since paid off, of course. "Blue" has appeared on every Green Day record and has been repaired and restored an incalculable number of times. When bands today try—and fail—to achieve that Green Day guitar sound, at once clean and, somewhere in the tone, a little broken and raw, what they're missing is "Blue" running through their Marshall amps.

•

Armstrong would soon draw even more post-tragedy comfort from an unlikier source.

Eleven-year-old Michael Ryan Pritchard, with his scrawny limbs, goofy grin, and blond bowl-cut hair, could barely cross a hall without injuring himself. He seemed to be one of those kids just wired for trouble, the kind who would find the one unchecked glass filled with staining liquid and knock it over with what seemed like radar-guided precision. Pritchard hardly possessed a set of clothes that fit, much less the solidity needed to fill the void left by the death of a parent, but he could make Armstrong laugh until his jaws ached. He and Billie Joe became instant friends that winter after meeting at Carquinez Middle School. During every lunch hour, the two bonded over music. Pritchard was into Van Halen, but turned Armstrong on to even darker hard rock, like Judas Priest and Iron Maiden.

The friends bonded over sadness as well. Born in Oakland, on May 4, 1972, Pritchard was given up by his birth mother, a Native American woman with a heroin addiction. At six weeks old, he was placed with Cheryl Nasser and Patrick

Pritchard, registered foster care parents who lived in El Sobrante, a suburb about five miles from Rodeo.

As Armstrong's was, Pritchard's early childhood was untroubled. Sharp and pointed, he excelled in school, despite frequently missing classes due to the various illnesses that may have been a result of his birth mother's condition.

Patrick was getting his degree at UC Berkeley while Cheryl stayed at home with Mike and his sister Mycla. But pressures and youth got the better of the couple, and soon they were fighting frequently.

Pritchard and his sister witnessed one particularly ugly verbal sparring that resulted in a call to the local police. Shortly thereafter Cheryl moved to Rodeo with Mycla, and Pritchard remained with Patrick in El Sobrante. But he missed his mother and soon followed her to Rodeo. Even as tensions between the Pritchards eased somewhat, Mike withdrew into himself. Once described as "fearless" by his mother, he was sullen and barely communicative when he first met Armstrong.

Even more than any empathetic bond, or love of semi-absurd British metal, Pritchard and Armstrong are connected in a way that seems oddly cosmic, as if they were two halves of one person.

"I think they just allow each other to be themselves," Anna Armstrong Humann says by way of explaining the bond. "There's no judgment. And it was easy to look at Mike and make fun of him. 'What a weirdo. Dresses funny. Hyper kid.' But I think Billie Joe just accepted him for who he was and Mike accepted Billie for the kid that he was."

Mike wasn't the musician that Billie was. He'd only recently shown an interest in guitar, but soon the pair would be logging hours in Armstrong's room with "Blue" and a handful of albums. "Mike really wanted to play guitar," David Armstrong says. "One day Billie had Mike over, and me and my buddies were about to go out for the night and we saw them sitting on me and Billie's bed, which I'd separated into twin beds by then. One was sitting on one side, and one was on the other. Billie was teaching Mike chords. That was about six o'clock. I got home at two o'clock in the morning, and they were still there. And Billie looked up at me and said, 'Hey, Dave, watch what Mike can do.' And Mike knew four or five songs from start to end. That's the connection they had. I don't think that Mike knew a note at the beginning of the night. But when I came home, he could play [Ozzy Osbourne's] 'Crazy Train,' and a couple of Van Halen songs. And he knew them well. That's the way they could communicate." Soon Mike was taking lessons with George Cole, and the afternoons became not only long jams, but song-writing sessions as well. The two boys provided each other with a confidence that had been seldom available and certainly unsustainable in both of their daily lives.

"There was a sense of freedom where no one is looking at you and no one is critiquing what you're doing," Armstrong explains. "And you don't have to better what you've done in the past because you don't have any past. It's the very beginning and you're just listening to everything for the first time and saying like 'Wow, look what I can do! Jesus Christ. Where the fuck is this coming from?'"

From the beginning, Armstrong and Pritchard's telepathy was evident in their "stage" chemistry. "I'd look over at him and know what to do," Pritchard once explained to the *Alternative Press*. Their shared, somewhat drill sergeant–like approach to rehearsals made them a tight unit even before they had any rhythm section. "We were always very diligent," Mike recalled. "When we weren't doing anything else, we were always practicing. Every day."

After leaving Carquinez Middle School, Mike attended Salesians High School, an all-boys Catholic school in nearby Richmond, California. Billie, like his brothers and sisters, entered John Swett High School in Crockett. John Swett was a small school, with a student body of around four hundred. In his early teens, while deriving an incredible sense of creative and emotional satisfaction from music, Armstrong had not yet devoted all his waking hours to this pursuit. Happily, he probably didn't even realize that he was conforming, as he embraced his inner semi-jock. Armstrong enjoyed sports.

"He once wrote that he wanted to be either a rock star or a professional football player when he grew up," David recalls. Billie was a strong swimmer and a quick runner. He played tailback in the local Pop Warner football little league but only made water boy at John Swett. David Armstrong was, like his dad, a big guy, and protected his little brother from any potential bullies who might take advantage of his size and sensitivity, but he couldn't protect Armstrong from poor taste. "I remember there was a talent show, and he lost to a bunch of football players doing a rap," David says, and laughs. "Big white linemen rapping. They won and even they told me, 'Man, your brother went up there and sang a song that he wrote!'" Poor sportsmanship was a factor as well. "I'd see him slam his helmet down on the field a couple of times [in frustration]," David recalls. Student life at John Swett and an acceptance of his own physical limitations would soon compel Billie Joe to forgo athletics entirely and embrace music with a fervor that was not only undiluted, it was now infused with an ambition beyond his years. If he wasn't going to score touchdowns, he would show all rhyme-busting jocks what he could really do.

By tenth grade, Armstrong, Pritchard, and their best friends Sean Hughes and Jason Relva would take advantage of Ollie's absence and the run of her house. "They weren't doing drugs in the house, but they did have a lot of freedom," David says. "Billie certainly had the most freedom of all of us kids." The instruments were soon moved from the bedroom out into the sitting room, where the four friends could jam loudly without anyone complaining. "We were the little Van Halen kids," Hughes says. "The little rocker kids. Mike had a guitar by then. Billie had his guitar, and one day he said to me, 'Why don't you play bass?' So I bought a bass. He basically told me what to do. 'Hey, play this. Now play this.'" For the first time, the friends started thinking about forming an actual group. "The goal for me was just fun," Hughes admits. "It was a lot cooler than band class. But for Billie, he was actually into making music. He wanted to put a band together to play his songs."

Armstrong played lead guitar, Mike played rhythm guitar, a local kid named Raj Punjabi was one of the more frequent semi-members who'd come in and play drums, and Jason Relva (whose tragic death in a 1992 car accident inspired the mid-nineties Green Day anthem "J.A.R.") would provide general support: an audience prototype. Band names flew around as frequently as botched notes. "We played a bunch of metal songs as Condom." Hughes laughs. "Then we called ourselves Desecrated Youth. Those songs were a bit more rock. I guess more punkish." Not that they'd know. While the early eighties hardcore that would later inspire them so completely was in its ascent, Armstrong, Pritchard, and Hughes were obliviously shredding heshers, complete with greasy hair, backward ball caps, concert tees, and Converse sneaks.

Mike Pritchard and Sean Hughes had transferred from Salesians High School to Pinole High in nearby Pinole (pronounced *pinol'*). Pinole High was the largest school in the area, with a racially and culturally diverse student body of about two thousand. Fed up with John Swett, Billie opportunistically used his big brother Allen's address to make himself eligible to follow his friends there. By eleventh grade, all three were enrolled, and the band had a permanent name: Sweet Children.

The band took their name from one of Billie Joe's very early originals. An improbably clean and sprightly example (given their penchant for sludge or arpeggio-laden heavy metal) of throwaway speed pop (with lyrics ostensibly about memories of childhood flirtations, when boys first start becoming interested in girls and vice verse), "Sweet Children" wasn't much of a song; but it was, for a little while at least, a good enough band name.

Drive past the one-level beige and maroon–painted Pinole High today and there is actually some solid evidence that a pair of punk rock superstars are alumni. Ground has been broken. Among the racially mixed student body, a few sourpuss teens loiter curbside, holding their skateboards close. Both girls and boys wear wallet chains, hoodies, checked nerd-shorts, and big clunky black boots. They will probably not be attending any Spartan pep rallies after school, but many of them, despite appearances, are well-adjusted and college-bound. They only look like burnouts. It's a lot less socially damning to affect an outcast air in 2006. In 1986, not so much.

"We got fucked with a lot at first," Sean Hughes recalls. "We called [the bullies] Pods. It stood for Pinole Oriented Dicks." Even worse, the friends were ignored by the cool kids and, more crucially, the girls. "We didn't have girlfriends," Hughes admits. "We tried. Crushes and stuff. You like a lot of girls and find out some of them don't like you. Some of them call you ugly. Some of them you put on your sniper's list the rest of your life. I always thought Billie was more charismatic than the rest of us, but even he pulled back a little more. We didn't come into ourselves until the Gilman scene, a bit later."

"I don't think anybody thought very much of them," remembers Robert Brown, a Pinole High classmate. "The crap I heard was not directed at them but like basically that whole group of people. 'Oh, they're just losers,'" he laughs. "They were nobody."

"In high school a lot of people were into these different things that I wasn't into at all anymore," Armstrong remembers. "Sports and cheerleading."

Both Armstrong and Pritchard attended classes when they had to—Pritchard was the more diligent student—but they both secretly considered the band's progression as their primary form of study. That and weed, anyway. In high school, Pritchard and Armstrong first learned that smoking pot made playing music even more interesting. Still, they were two of the most ambitious stoners who ever inhaled. "They were always trying to get my brother and me to see them play," Brown continues. " 'Oh, come listen to our band.' They finally played at school so I saw them then. It was Foreign Foods Day, they called it. They had exotic food and a couple bands play. Sweet Children were one of them. They all played in the quad. Out in the middle of the school. I remember liking them. But most of the people that were really paying attention to them were the other few punks at our school. The jocks and everyone else didn't care."

Billie Joe was slowly being primed to embrace the punk-rock scene he was about to enter. Anna was a huge fan of "college rock," pre-Nirvana alternative hitmakers who really made no hits (not yet, anyway) but whose influence was already wide and massive.

"Billie got introduced to Hüsker Dü and the Replacements by his sister," Hughes says. "And I remember going to a 10,000 Maniacs show with them. That was pretty different. Natalie Merchant." It was an R.E.M. show in Santa Cruz (about an hour's drive from Rodeo) in 1985 that really opened him up. "It was the *Fables of the Reconstruction* tour," Armstrong told me in a 2005 *Spin* interview "Michael Stipe had a shaved head and wore an old overcoat. I thought, 'This is different.' "

"I left him alone at that show." Anna laughs. "I said 'I gotta go stand in front of Peter Buck, so I'll see you later.' And he ended up hanging out with these punk-rock kids there. You know, with bleached hair and different clothes, and they pushed him up to the front of the stage. I think it really helped him and changed his life about music." As he did with Allen's Beatles albums, Billie Joe began studying his sister's college rock, sitting for hours with a Camper Van Beethoven or Replacements cassette and "Blue." He taught himself the Replacements' "If Only You Were Lonely," and it soon joined Chuck Berry's "Johnny B. Goode" as the highlight of Sweet Children's set list. Not that the band was following up Foreign Foods Day with a world tour or anything. They were still drummer-less . . . and they had homework. But they also had this thing called punk rock, and it was about to change the way they saw the world. To be a punk was to declare yourself an outsider. Pritchard and Armstrong certainly felt as much at Pinole. Happily, there were others who shared these feelings. You could be an outsider with real back-up.

"There was a core group of people that I found felt the same way (that I did)," Armstrong says. "We were the suburban punks."

"I remember them being real quiet at first," Brown says. "Every time I saw them after that, they'd be hanging out with his group (of people)." "We were gunning to be different by then," Sean Hughes recalls. "Punk-rock attire. Punk-rock attitude."

When they hung out with the Pinole High punks (realistically fewer than two dozen kids), Billie and Mike felt as if they had their own group. They could compete with the jocks and the brains. It didn't matter who had more money or better grades. The music was exciting, more so than heavy metal anyway. There was no going back to solo Ozzy after Hüsker Dü or Bad Brains. In a 1992 interview with *Flipside,* Armstrong confessed that he felt a little like a wimp in hindsight after comparing this new punk music he was into while at Pinole with the glossy pop metal he'd been listening to at home. "Sometimes I listen to those bands now and the guitar sound isn't quite as full," he recalls. "But back then, it was like 'Wow, that's amazing!' Now I listen to it and it sounds kind of wimpy."

Punk dress and attitude got them attention or notoriety where they otherwise risked fading into the background.

One night, in a burst of enthusiasm for this new thing in his life, Pritchard shaved his head into a lopsided Mohawk. He spiked it up with some shaving cream and admired himself in the mirror of his mother's bedroom. He wouldn't be able to sport it for long, however. The Pritchards were having financial trouble, so Mike got an after-school job as a sous-chef at a seafood restaurant in nearby Crockett called the Nantucket. He would constantly reek like fish, but after a few months, he'd saved enough money to eventually purchase a used pickup truck, which made it that much easier to follow this newly discovered culture wherever it was taking root. And in the winter of 1987, that meant Berkeley. There, in a cold graffiti-strewn space in the city's Western warehouse district, Sweet Children would learn what can be done with these new feelings of enlightened outsiderism. "There was this kid named Eggplant that first told us about what was going on at Gilman," says Hughes. "His real name was Robert Burnett. Why did they call him Eggplant? Damned if I know. He was from Pinole, and his sister Phaedra was friends with my sister, so he was over one night and Billie and Mike happened to be there and he was talking about Gilman and these great bands like Isocracy and how we should check it out. Billie was more intrigued by it than I was at first. He really held an ear to him that night."

Chapter Two

THE GILMAN STREET PROJECT

Before 924 Gilman Street opened on New Year's Day, 1987, the Bay Area was not the most welcoming place for a lasting punk scene to take hold. Even in the late seventies, when punk was the rave in New York, Los Angeles, and London, the region had the only semblance of a local movement. That the early San Francisco punks largely copied what they interpreted from somewhat exploitational television news magazine profiles and editorials to be a punk way of dressing and behaving says much about the initial lack of identity.

"The Sex Pistols were on *60 Minutes* [on the eve of their U.S. tour in 1978]," recalls Dirk Dirksen, a veteran of local theater and television productions, who would go on to promote and emcee the area's formative punk shows. "The very next day you'd see the change in appearances. The longhairs cut their hair off and started wearing safety pins."

"Whereas New York people looked more like the Ramones or Television or Blondie or something," remembers Jello Biafra, former leader of the area's most famous early punk act, the Dead Kennedys, "San Francisco was the first place in the United States where most of the people were sporting the British spiky hair and chains and pins." Biafra carefully adds,

"This shouldn't suggest that there were even enough punks to constitute a scene early on."

"It seemed like the Haight was pretty dead," Penelope Houston, who fronted another influential local act, the Avengers, says. "There was the Warfield and Winterland but those were venues for major, major bands. The Tubes were around; they were kind of the reigning band of San Francisco at that moment. But pretty soon after I arrived in 1977, I started noticing strange bands playing around this place called the Mabuhay Gardens."

The Mabuhay Gardens was a red velvet–draped Filipino social club located on Broadway in the seedier section of the city's North Beach area. "The neighborhood had gone topless," Dirksen remembered. When he first approached the club's owners about using the stage, he was intent on providing a venue for the local underground theater movement but quickly discovered there were three times as many nascent punk acts than avant garde theater troupes who were eager to perform. "We figured these people deserved a venue as much as anyone," Dirksen says.

The Mabuhay (or "Mab," as it was referred to by most) served food and therefore was technically a restaurant open to all ages. Attracted by great local acts like The Nuns, Crime, Flipper, and the aforementioned Avengers, the club became the nucleus for exciting Bay Area rock 'n' roll. When the Sex Pistols themselves came to town on January 14th of '78 to perform what would be their last concert ever (until their 1996 and 2003 reunions anyway) at the Winterland Ballroom, hippie-era mega-promoter Bill Graham stacked the bill with Mabuhay bands. "He wanted to make sure he could fill it," Dirksen says, laughing. "So he booked The Nuns, Crime, and the Avengers." Graham's relationship with local punks was condescendingly cordial at best.

"Oh, he was very hostile to punk underground, and the punk underground was hostile to him in return," Biafra confirms. "The reason being that the guy wanted to control everything. He couldn't stand the thought of any other promoter letting any band play even if it was in somebody's bathroom. There were a lot of police raids on non–Bill Graham venues, especially punk rock shows."

The surprise success of the Mabuhay inspired a few dozen smaller punk venues, both public and private, to open throughout the Bay Area. "There were some cool little places," remembers local artist Winston Smith (who designed sleeves for the Dead Kennedys and later for Green Day's *Insomniac* album). "One was called the Deaf Club; it actually was a space for deaf people. But they liked the punk scene there because they could actually hear the music by putting their fingers on the table. They probably thought they were listening to Guy Lombardo or something. But at least it was something they could hear because the vibrations went straight to the wood. There was The Sound of Music; there was a place called the Zone. A place called Tool and Die that was great, it was just in someone's basement on Valencia, I believe. And a place called the Farm, which had actually been a communal farm and had kind of been turned into a big auditorium."

Ironically—since most punks seem to have an avowed hatred of all things "hippie"—the communal/radical spirit of the Bay Area progenitors such as the original Beats (who congregated at the City Lights bookstore in North Beach) and the Haight Street Dead-heads was eagerly and gratefully picked up by the first wave of spike-haired punk rockers. "If you strip away the thin veneer of punk in the Bay Area scene, there was always a hippie undercurrent," observes Dr. Frank Portman, who would go on to front the Mr. T. Experience, one of the first, and certainly one of the most fun, acts from the early 924 Gilman Street wave.

"When me and my weird friends first got out of high school and were able to jump in, it seemed like the radical side of 'long hair as a rebellious statement' and all that went with it was evaporating," Biafra remembers. "And we were heartbroken. 'Oh my God, we were born too late; we missed the sixties!' But when punk hit I thought, 'Oh wait a minute, I was born at the perfect time.' Even the older folks from the Beat generation like Bruce Connor, the filmmaker and photographer, jumped right into the punk scene because he liked the energy. And Allen Ginsberg put up the money for the first issue of *Search and Destroy*."

Search and Destroy was a monthly 'zine published out of San Francisco; thanks to consistently sharp writing and an influential cluttered type, cut-and-paste design style, it soon found a wider audience among punks in major cities, colleges, and smaller enclaves across the world. Proto-punk acts such as Roky Erikson and the Flaming Groovies were celebrated, along with non-musician honorary punks including filmmakers David Lynch, John Waters, and Russ Meyer, or writers like J. G. Ballard and William S. Burroughs. Local labels could stay alive through ads and mail order, and local bands were given a forum as well.

"The San Francisco scene was more intelligence-driven and more political in part because the main 'zine was *Search and Destroy*," Biafra continues. "Which kind of dared people to come up with interesting things to say in the interviews. Still the best punk 'zine I've seen to this day."

Along with Los Angeles–based *Flipside* (which also began in 1977), *Maximumrocknroll* (*MRR*) ranks as the most influential punk 'zine of them all. *MRR* began as a local radio show hosted by a transplanted Northeasterner named Tim Yohannan. Yohannan was raised in Northern New Jersey and attended Rutgers in the late sixties. "We were war protesters together," says Lenny Kaye, also a Rutgers student. "Was he a socialist then? Yeah probably. But so was I."

Yohannan's father, John David Yohannan, was a former U.S. Air Corps officer during World War II. He was eventually named a Professor Emeritus of English and comparative literature at City College in New York. He's the author of *Treasury of Asian Literature,* which remains in print fifty years since its publication. "I visited him at his parents' house once," Kaye says. "We sat there and listened to Moby Grape's first record, and I noticed that he had a very interesting habit. He liked to cover the sides of his albums in green tape. I don't know why."

Despite having an academic father figure with military experience, Yohannan was a natural born agitator and organizer. "Toward the end of our senior year, we were in the anti-ROTC demonstration together," Kaye continues. "We were both suspended and had to do community service so we could graduate. Tim told me in later years he wished he'd just told them to go 'Fuck off' and not done it."

Having just turned thirty, Yohannan was a good ten years older than the audience of punk rock kids who devoured the loud, fast, and difficult to find tracks from local and international punk acts. The fact that his audience probably scratched their heads at the radical polemics that he and his DJ crew Ruth Schwartz and Jeff Bale spouted on air didn't seem to matter. Yohannan knew these were hungry ears, and he was going to fill them as he saw fit. It would be good for them in the long run should anything sink in, he reasoned.

MRR was taped and shared across the country and eventually officially syndicated. Some of those very tapes would later find their way into the hands of suburban punks like Billie Joe, Mike, and their Pinole High School friends: the Dead Kennedys, Black Flag, the Germs, and Flipper blasting out of sticker-customized boom boxes and car stereos in suburban parking lots state-wide. The success of the radio show encouraged the publication of the 'zine. Its original look was, also like *Search and Destroy,* cluttered and Xeroxed black-and-white type, smudgy photos, and lots of cartoons. Its tone: gossipy, catty, but always self-serious.

"Tim was just trying to have a magazine that showed what

the real underground punk scene was about—in terms of political culture anyway," remembers Fat Mike, of Southern California pop-punk favorites NOFX (and founder of indie label Fat Wreck Chords). "I read it then, and I still read it. I like the news section. The columns. They kept you apprised of what was going on in the underground. Plus Tim was one of the few people there who didn't hate my band. We went to Sizzler together a couple of times. Tim loved Sizzler."

"The magazine was a real important thing in that world, genuinely important," Dr. Frank Portman agrees. "Like everybody read it. The scene reports were avidly read."

"I wrote three or four of these missives from Portland," remembers early *MRR* contributor Courtney Love. "All about Poison Idea and Rancid Vat. But of course being me, I wrote something controversial and got a cross burned on my lawn. I wrote that Tom 'Pig' [Tom 'Pig Champion' Roberts, leader of cult heroes Poison Idea] was a neo-fascist or something."

"Tim was the emperor of the *MRR* empire," Portman explains. "It was first among equals. He was living out his counterculture ideals. You live [at the offices], you work there, and he was against paying anybody. Everybody had to have at least a part-time job. I cannot speak for them, but from what I remember, Tim had the hippie background, but the ethos that was formed by him and his generation got solidified into this aggregate of pseudo-political clichés. Self-conscious ideas of rebellion against society and anti-capitalism. The [MRR] aesthetic grew out of the darker counterculture, where you dressed in black and you said 'fuck' a lot and you had Che Guevara shirts and you were into Patty Hearst and that kind of world, which is a very Bay Area thing. That was the old guard and the punks became their followers. Tim really saw himself as a corruptor of the young in the best possible sense."

Yohannan was a self-righteous fighter by nature and for anyone with that personality type it's useful to have a nemesis. In 1981 Ronald Reagan was sworn in as the fortieth president of the United States. Reagan quickly became the target for all of the new wave of hard-core's rage, virtually fueling the entire movement.

"I went to a *lot* of Rock Against Reagan shows," remembers Fat Mike. In the Reagan era, the fashion punks and borderline New Wavers were simply not committed enough to fight the good fight. Reagan was blamed for everything that was wrong with the Bay Area. If it was a dilemma, Ronnie had a hand in it.

"The people walking around [the Bay Area] talking to themselves; we all blamed on Ronald Reagan," remembers David Katznelson (then Bay Area punk who later became a Warner Brothers A-and-R executive and producer). "It was his cutbacks of the institutions that housed these people, the halfway houses that threw them all onto the streets."

The anger was palpable. Punk soon became a synonym for being enlightened and ready to pledge yourself to the resistance. It used to mean you'd smash windows and sniff glue. Now it meant your eyes were open. You were sober. You were (most likely) a white Black Panther. You were a radical with a shaved head, and a healthy, drug-free body covered in a utilitarian T-shirt. Maybe you had rich parents to facilitate your stance. Maybe you had a pocket full of change from panhandling because capitalism was lame. Punk fundamentalism was born in the post-Reagan age. And, ironically, along with it came punk-oversensitivity syndrome. It was the era of the touchy punk. Armstrong and Pritchard were not even old enough to vote, and yet they were obliged to be aware, merely by commuting into the city, and stretching out their hands to be "X-ed" with an all-ages brand.

"I was thinking these hard-core punks were like little old ladies," jokes Portman. "They can't stand to hear a song that is not about El Salvador. Sometimes I'd say, 'This song is about El Salvador; no I'm just kidding.' It was a weird scene. You'd get challenged for your attitudes. I bet it probably was like that in Washington, DC, as well. In San Francisco, it was political correctness in the punk scene from top to bottom. You can adopt that iconography, however, and those clichés and make good rock 'n' roll.

The Mabuhay Garden's upstairs room, a theater space known as the On Broadway, soon became a showcase for the more aggressive and faster mutation of second-wave punk (known as hard-core). These hard-core shows started to attract an even younger crowd than the early Mabuhay bills. As punk grew, the number of kids coming in from the outer suburbs expanded as well. It was inside the On Broadway that many of the *MRR*-reading high school kids, who would make up the first wave of 924 Gilman Street bands, first congregated.

"We went there every single weekend to see these bands and got a pretty good education in what it was all about," Portman says. "There was another place called the Vat because it had all these old beer vats. We played there. It was really associated with this band Condemned 2 Death because I think they lived there. So you were a 'Vat rat' if you hung out at the Vat."

Some hard-core kids never went back to the suburbs. They'd stay in the city, squatting on corners, panhandling, and tweaking out on the biker speed that soon became the chosen drug. The scene was not for everyone but it did finally achieve its own identity in the eighties.

"It was dirty; it was skanky," says Courtney Love, who spent some time on the nascent hard-core scene before moving to Minneapolis. "I went out with a guy who ran the Tool and Die but going all the way over to Berkeley on the BART [Bay Area Rapid Transit]? Forget it. Too much panhandling for me. I was a new waver. There was no romance to it. No place for girls. No place for the kind of boys I liked. The stench of beer. The smell of the speed labs and the little alleys. I can't even go to San Francisco now because it reminds me of that."

For every dropout punk squatter, there was an MRRer pledged to construct. "*Maximumrocknroll* did something that was almost unheard of from the moment they started publishing," Biafra points out. "They came out every month right when they said they were going to and that was because Tim knew how to stay organized and crack a whip."

"I thought Tim was this champion of this kind of punk rock music that I secretly didn't particularly like, which was hard-core, and I learned later that he really hated hard-core too," Portman laughs. "But he believed that it was the way to attract the youth to his cause. He knew a potential when he saw it and so he got involved. At that point, it started to get actually organized."

"By the time the Gilman Scene started, the shock of the new was probably starting to wear off of punk," Houston observes, explaining the necessary cultural segue from classic punk into utilitarian, and often Socialist, hard-core. "I mean, I try to explain to people what it was like walking around San Francisco with blue hair and people's jaws dropping and stuff. By the eighties there didn't seem to be any danger in it. There didn't seem to be any of the original cultural shock. It seemed to be more, to me, of a high school or teenage expression. And I don't want to place any judgment on the value of that to anybody, but it didn't have any bite as far as I was concerned. I was sort of over it. The East Bay was not happening at all in the seventies. Maybe there were a couple of bands from there [playing in San Francisco] but not much was really happening on that side. But then in the eighties . . ."

A large city to the east of San Francisco, Berkeley has a long history of providing a haven for the counter culture: creative firebrands from Allen Ginsberg to author Phillip K. Dick to cartoonist R. Crumb to filmmakers Francis Ford Coppola and George Lucas to Black Panther Huey P. Newton to heiress turned guerilla Patty Hearst. Still, in the early eighties, with the exception of some on-campus parties at the University of

California, there weren't that many punk rock shows. But as the On Broadway scene expanded, promoters and bands searched for venues on the other side of the Bay out of necessity.

"Before Gilman opened, we started putting on shows at this pizza place called Owns Pizza in Berkeley," Portman says. "Owns Pizza was the beginning of the whole Gilman thing. Basically, we were all setting up shows in places like that. Pizza places."

After a point, the idea that the city was a perfect place for a permanent punk venue, where Bill Graham had no pull and the surplus of garage-practicing punk acts throughout the Bay Area could have a reliable, safe, and clean environment to play, took off. There would always be punks as long as there were teenagers. Why float around from venue to venue and deal with each attendant hassle from the owners or the cops or the neighbors? Why not have something that would stand for years?

It would be at 924 Gilman where this idealism and the pop melodic punk of the Ramones and the politicized early hardcore of the the Dead Kennedys (and touring acts like Black Flag, the Bad Brains, and Minor Threat) would collide violently to create a new sound and a new ethos, both of which would heavily influence Green Day in their formative years.

"There would not have been a Gilman Street scene without Tim's organizational skills," Biafra says. "He was about the only guy in the whole scene who could keep a schedule and motivate other people to get things done on time."

"*MRR* came to us for advice," Dirk Dirksen says. "[The Mabuhay] was closing after a ten-year run, and they were the new thing happening. So they asked us, 'How do you book bands? How do you run a sound system?' It was very methodical."

Once you cross the San Francisco–Oakland Bay Bridge and put the hills behind you, there's not much to indicate that anything historic has ever transpired on tree-lined Gilman Street. There are no bronze plaques or statues. Industrious sorts have not made any effort to capitalize on 924 Gilman's legacy: no skate shop or independent record store. Just a few trading posts and a NO WAR sign in a small pet shop window to indicate that this strip was, and still is, a hub for politically charged punk rock. Visit Gilman Street during the day, and you'll hear loud, circling gulls by the vast trash collection yard. There will be garbage stink and salt water vapor blowing over the hot pavement as you walk toward Eighth Street. But you may also notice that each telephone pole is littered with staple gun scars and brand-new gig flyers. Gilman remains a stop on any van-touring punk band's itinerary, and any night of the week, you'll still see four or five of them on a bill. As it approaches its twentieth year of existence it continues to be faithful to the vision of its founders. This collective, spear-headed by Yohannan, always conceived of Gilman as some-thing that would not merely open and close, as so many other punk venues. Gilman was not something that would burn it-self out or be shut down by the city over a line of ignored fine print. From the early planning stages, Gilman was con-structed to last.

"Every punk club always goes for a while and then gets shut down. Tim's whole thing was 'We're gonna create this club and it's going to be solid. Totally cool with the city, all the right permits, drug- and alcohol-free place,'" remembers Jesse Michaels, at the time a politically minded Bad Brains fan, who would later cofound and front the scene's most influ-ential band: Operation Ivy.

While it would not be uncommon for a gang of punks to simply take over something like a broken down, abandoned raw space and squat there till the cops or the conditions forced them out, Yohannan approached the entire project as if he were opening a supermarket. Zoning law books were opened. Neighborhoods were canvassed for local support. It was old-fashioned politicking, and it succeeded in easing the punk-wary community. Something radical was coming, but it would be positive and it would be completely legal.

Around the fall of 1986 flyers began circulating locally, asking passersby:

> "Isn't it time we created a real alternative: A diverse group of Bay Area fanzines, Musicians, Artists, and active members of the alternative scene have come together to create a new environment. It is being built by and for those who become involved in making it happen. A warehouse has been leased by *Maximumrocknroll* and a democratic structure has been organized to operate a community center. The necessary permits have been attained from the city of Berkeley, and construction has begun. This promises to be an exciting center for a wide range of music, art, cultural, and educational activities."

Ads were taken out in the back sections of *MRR* as well, announcing 924 Gilman's existence, conceptually at least. Operation Ivy cofounder Tim Armstrong, a Bay Area native, had been unable to keep a band together on the local scene for a few years. Bored with his part-time job at Berkeley pizza parlor Fat Slice, he decided to relocate to New York City where local hard-core acts like the Cro Mags and Murphy's Law seemed infinitely more exciting. "It just seemed like the thing to do. If I liked New York, my plan was to stay there. I didn't really know anyone," Armstrong says. "All I wanted to do was roam the streets of the Lower East Side. That night I hit my first shows at CBGB. The Gorilla Biscuits and Youth of Today. Afterward everyone hung out for hours talking outside about music and stuff going on in their lives. I remember wishing the East Bay had a spot like CB's. The next day, I was hanging out at a fanzine shop on St. Marks Place, reading *MRR,* and I came across an ad about a new club opening in

Berkeley. When I saw that ad, I knew I had to go home. Looking back now, if it wasn't for that ad, I would have stayed in Manhattan. I'm sure of it. Sometimes it takes one little thing to make up my mind and get me going. I was soon headed back to the East Bay on another three-day Greyhound bus ride."

Creating a genuine sense of excitement over something major and valuable seemed designed to make the hours of difficult physical and administrative work bearable (and inspired a much-needed infusion of material donations). "My father was a general contractor at the time, and he donated materials [to Gilman]," Dr. Portman says. "*MRR* organized the club the way you organize a commune."

There were rumors that Yohannan and the 'zine contributed $40,000 of their own money to cover outstanding costs and ensure that the club would open sooner than later. Where the money came from (if it did in fact come from him personally), remains part of the Yohannan myth. "I heard various rumors about Tim having money from somewhere," Jesse Michaels says. "He worked a union job. But he had a huge house in San Francisco. Gilman Street cost a shitload of money and I don't really know where it came from. I've also heard things like that he was actually funded by the Communist Party, which sounds to me preposterous. But it's one of the things I heard. I don't really know where the dough came from."

The club was officially approved by the City of Berkeley on New Year's Eve 1986 and opened to the public that same day.

"The first Gilman Show was Christ on Parade playing with Soup," Tim Armstrong remembers. "I went down there with [future Operation Ivy bass player] Matt Freeman to check it out, and I felt at home as soon as I walked into the place. There was no backstage. It was a punk club run by punks. There was no sense of hierarchy at all. Things were equal. I was overwhelmed. It was as exciting as the first time I picked up a Ramones album. I felt something magical was happening again, but this time I was in the middle of it."

Once operational, members were obliged to pay dues and attend weekly meetings designed to keep the inner workings efficient and faithful to the original ethic.

"Sunday afternoons," Portman recalls, with a shudder. "It was just the widest cross-section of people," remembers Jesse Michaels. "People in their fifties. And people who were like fourteen. Hippies and punks. It was pretty cool. But there were *so* many meetings. Organizing. You know, socialists just love to have meetings."

"Everybody went," Portman says. "And the reason you went is that you wanted to be involved so your band could play there because there was nowhere else to play. I'd go and I'd be doing a crossword puzzle or reading a book, and they would have these crazy arguments. They'd discuss booking. Everyone wanted to be in booking, but Tim didn't want to make it elite; you know, every committee is equal. You have to prove your worth to be in the booking committee. And of course, you wanted to be on the booking committee if you had a band for obvious reasons. Then there was security. The security committee would discuss how can we have noncoercive security? They had lots of proposals that would range from 'Well does anyone know karate?' This one guy Brian Edge stood up at one of those meetings and said, 'Well, I have a real problem with forcing myself upon another human being.' I just lost it. For much of the meetings, I was just on the verge of cracking up the whole time."

Eventually a noncoercive security method was proposed, although it was exceedingly difficult in practice. If someone started trouble, the security patrol people would place their own hands behind their backs and, en masse, nudge the troublemaker out of the club with their bellies. "I guess the hands behind the back symbolized some sort of strength through weakness thing," Portman mused.

Although Billie Joe Armstrong was short and Mike Pritchard was scrawny, both of them happily volunteered to help with security to attend shows there. Luckily, there was never an incident. Both teens were mainstays from opening day onward. "We lived and died for that place," Pritchard remembered. "At the time, it meant everything."

Armstrong and Pritchard studied the stage presence and song structure of each Gilman band with a precision their high school teachers never observed. It was their higher education, closer to home than San Francisco, and with a little hands-behind-the-back patrolling, it was affordable.

As exciting as it was to be in the city, unprotected, free, wide-eyed, and frequently stoned, unlike some of their punk-rock peers, they always returned to Rodeo. Jobs and school and band practice could not be abandoned, as exhilarating as these weekend rallies were. However, they took with them these spiritually invigorating new thoughts: Reagan is bad. Socialism can work. Speed is intense. Queers are radical. Reagan is *really* bad. Maybe I should be a vegetarian? (That last one is especially troubling when your mother works in a barbecue joint. Armstrong would eventually eliminate meat from his diet, but at the time, he ate the food his mother put on the table.) Exposure to Gilman was like mainlining a multivitamin cocktail after over a dozen years of cultural malnutrition.

"Sometimes I'd drive him there, and come back and pick him and Mike up," Anna Armstrong Humann says. "And Billie would tell me all about it. That was really when he separated himself from the family. And not in the sense that he didn't have anything to do with us. It just changed his values and shaped his lifestyle and how he saw himself. How he saw the world. It changed the type of people he wanted to be around. He'd found a community that he wanted to be a part of."

Plus . . . there were interested girls there. Almost immediately, Billie discovered that the way he was being perceived by women was wildly different from the way it was in Rodeo or Pinole. He hadn't changed—not physically, anyway. The values had. Talent was sexy, no matter what you looked like. And being a little left of center no longer made you a loser. Outside of suburbia, when the xenophobia ceded to tolerance, it was a cool badge: something to be proud of.

Billie found his first serious girlfriend, Erica Paleno (who now spells her name Arica), inside Gilman when both were only sixteen. "People had to drive us to see each other," Paleno recalls with a laugh. Like Billie, Paleno was already a passionate rock 'n' roll fan, and the intuitive feelings she had about her new boyfriend were confirmed once he played her some of the four-track recordings that he'd made with Mike and Sean. "I guess I was one of the early people who thought that they had the potential to be big," she says. "I knew at a very young age that he was sort of a McCartney type. McCartney's a bass player, but I'm talking about being prolific . . . and writing those melodies. Whatever the formula is, the grand plan or the DNA that makes up that type of person, Billie is one of them. I'm fascinated and attracted to talent, and that's what it was for me. Because nobody thought he was a super hot guy at sixteen, that's for sure."

Billie Joe and Erica Paleno took advantage of the freedoms brought on by Ollie's long hours at Rod's Hickory Pit. While Mike was laboring over fish dinners, the two spent hours in Billie's room, making out and playing music. Paleno was the first in a trio of muses that would inspire some of Green Day's greatest songs. "I would steal his notebooks, his lyric books," she confesses. "I still have them, but they're tucked away. There's the original version of 'Christie Road' [which eventually appeared on Green Day's second full-length album, *Kerplunk!*], which he wrote for my mom and me. It's about meeting him at the train tracks and sneaking out of the house because my mom didn't let me. I was always grounded." Whenever they could get a ride to and from Berkeley (when not grounded, that is), they'd hit Gilman and feel that excitement and sense of belonging as soon as they passed through the doorway. "We thought it was so broad-based and open-minded for people who were outsiders like us," Paleno says. Those outsiders, however, were expected to work for their sense of belonging.

Perhaps Yohannan's most notorious suggestion was that bands, no matter how popular, had to work the club to play. Although none of the bands I interviewed for this book has any recollection of cleaning toilets, that function quickly became emblematic of Gilman's abolition of the rock 'n' roll caste system. There was to be no special treatment inside Gilman's walls. Whether they sucked or rocked, drew one hundred kids or ten kids, all bands were equal, and had to work for the privilege of playing there.

Headliners would not make any more or less money than the six or seven bands they'd played after. The fact that not any band but dozens of bands, with names like Wimpy Dicks, Vomit Launch, Rabid Lassie, Bulimia Banquet, Fuck Bubble, I Am the Hamster, Nasal Sex, and Child Support still clamored to play was, if nothing else, a testament to Yohannon's conviction and charisma.

"Some of the ideas were really stupid," Jesse Michaels says. "There were long arguments about whether or not they were going to have advertising. It's such a lefty thing. They wanted people to come even if it wasn't a good band. They wanted people to check out opening bands. A lot of it was just absurd."

"They would have these kind of tribunals that were sort of watered down Maoist practiced self-criticism where the ascenders would be in chairs in the middle of a circle of Gilman people, trying to account to themselves," Portman claims, "Tim's kind of pathetic version of being the head of a dictatorship of the punk proletariat. [The tribunals] were called Attitude Adjustment. Later, they just switched their name to Attitude."

Eventually, as will happen, the kids became a little frustrated with their mentors. Sometimes, especially when there's loud rock 'n' roll, you just want to feel free and escape. "It was divisive," Michaels says. "A lot of punks thought it was bullshit. There were too many rules, and it was too PC. There was an attitude of 'Fuck that place' after a while. I leaned toward the progressive side of the punk rock spectrum, but at the same time sometimes it got ridiculous. Someone would overhear someone saying something racist in the club and then there'd be a meeting about it the next day. It was just absurd."

Even touring bands passing through the Bay Area to play Gilman weren't spared these edicts. "They were liberals. And there's no shortage of rules on the left," says Brett Gurewitz, then of L.A. punk heroes Bad Religion and who'd later found the powerful indie rock label Epitaph Records. "It's actually the right that likes to abolish rules. People forget that. Socialism has rules up the ass. It was a little bit imposing. As a band, coming in there to play, I had the flu and we were on tour and I was in a van. We'd just driven eight hours to get there. And I was sitting on the stage with a fever and some guy came up to me and said, 'Everyone out. We need to kick everyone out, and only the people who can get their hands stamped can come back in.' I said, 'I just got here, I'm exhausted, and I'm in the band. Can't I just stay here?' 'Nope, you gotta get out like everyone else.' They said something about my rock star attitude."

Even odder than forcing touring bands to abide by Gilman rules was the unspoken policy of frostiness toward people who came from across the bridge. Insularity can only be harmful to a collective; but if a hard-core Gilman-er caught a whiff of a San Franciscan, much less one who was fresh from college and who may have a Volvo or a new Beamer parked somewhere up the road, the visitor might be well advised to take cover from a barrage of attitude. According to Gina Arnold, then-columnist for *BAM* magazine (the Bay Area weekly music paper), "The whole Gilman Street scene hated me. And I was never quite clear on that one. I just wasn't part of their gang. I was out of college. I was somebody from out of town [San Francisco], although I grew up in the Bay Area. The whole university thing wasn't their scene at all. So I was just sort of a convenient person for them not to like. I championed quite a few of the bands they liked [in my column], but that just made them hate me more. 'We love Fugazi. You can't come.' I see it now as a kind of joke but at the time it seemed very real to me."

Perhaps the most divisive policy of all was the no drugs or alcohol policy that enabled 924 Gilman to get up and running so quickly in the first place. People gave up drinking and getting high temporarily to see shows at the venue, and they'd say it was worth it; but for many it wasn't an easy sacrifice. "I'm definitely an alcoholic," Jeff Ott of the Bay Area punk band Crimpshrine confesses, "but I didn't feel like I was gonna miss coming to this club, which is really the only thing going, because I couldn't handle three hours without having a beer in my hand. You know, there was nothing about you that couldn't be loaded here; it was just you couldn't physically get loaded here."

For some reason, the only beverage available inside Gilman (besides water) was a locally bottled soda pop called Hansen's. Unlike Coke or Pepsi, this was the punk-approved soft drink. Still, there were many punks who secretly preferred something a little harder with their drums, bass, guitar, and volume. "There was a liquor store nearby," Portman says, "and there was Picante, a Mexican restaurant down the street, which is where I spent most of the Gilman shows that I played at except for the brief time I was onstage. I think you will hear many other bands express the same thing. I challenge anyone to manage hanging out in that place for six hours, which is how long the shows lasted, I challenge anyone to do that without at least some help."

The no drugs and alcohol policy within the club is most likely responsible for the somewhat erroneous image Bay Area punks have of being total joyless straight-edgers (probably akin to assuming that everyone who ever went to a Minor Threat show in DC pledged abstinence, or anyone who purchased more than one Smiths album was immediately a celibate or a vegetarian). "To this day I get kids all over America going, 'Oh, all you were straight-edge and vegetarian,'" Ott says, laughing. "And we always tell them, 'No, we just wanted to have a club where there wasn't a bar. And we didn't have to deal with the city and the police.'"

The friction between the *MRR* punks and the more hedonistic ones eventually became too much for Yohannan to deal with. In 1988, just a little more than a year after the doors opened, the magazine divested itself from Gilman. After closing its doors for a few weeks, the lease for the Gilman Street building was passed on to new owners and briefly renamed the Alternative Music Foundation (although to this day, nobody's ever referred to it as such).

Although much less militaristic, the original ideals of the Gilman Street club remain indivisible from the music and the public perception of the Berkeley punk scene. Yohannan, who died of cancer in 1998, has become synonymous with punk rock idealism: There is a genuine alternative way of living. Yohannan achieved what he intended to do. Even posthumously, he molds young minds. "We were at every fucking show from the very beginning," Tim Armstrong said. "I'd be playing basketball with Tim Yohannan before the show, dancing to my friends' bands during the show, and cleaning up the place at the end of the night. I felt like it was mine. My place. For once I felt like I was with a tribe of my own. My whole life, I was an outsider, a misfit, but at Gilman, I could be myself. I could say what I wanted to say, dress how I wanted to dress, and play the music that I loved."

"Tim actually put his idealism to real social use," Lenny

Kaye observes. "His collective there was based around music, but it was a real collective. And that's something that's given lip service to rather than actually put into practice. To this day, you have these mutant kids who don't really have a place in the world. You're not like an intellectual. You're not a sports guy. You're not anything, but you feel some sense of drive and expression building within you, and you need a place to check it out. That's what Tim founded at Gilman Street. A place where kids could come and meet like-minded human beings and form bands—one of the greatest social inventions known to man beyond marriage."

Chapter Three

LOOKOUT!

In 1987, Armstrong and Pritchard were welcome to attend punk shows at Gilman Street, but they had no luck as far as getting a slot even low on a bill for Sweet Children. Yohannan had heard their homemade tapes and dismissed them as simply "not punk enough."

There were other obstacles in Sweet Children's way. Mike's mother, under pressure to raise a family as a single parent for a while, finally decided that they would have to leave Rodeo. Faced with the prospect of losing the only thing in their lives that mattered before they even had a chance to really perform, the pair conspired to come up with ways for Mike to remain local. Billie Joe finally asked his mother if it would be possible for Mike to stay with them for a while. Perhaps he could live in the garage, which Andy had long ago converted into a homey space. Ollie sensed this was more than a whim. She liked Mike, who always took care to check his spastic impulses and act respectfully around her. At the start of their junior year at Pinole, Mike's mother and sister left Rodeo and he stayed behind. He and Billie Joe were brotherly, and now they lived like actual brothers. The close proximity enabled them to devote even more time to the band: specifically, how to penetrate 924 Gilman's punk-patrolled borders. There was only one small issue:

"His room reeked of fish," Anna Armstrong Humann laughs. "But he worked hard and he took care of himself. When his mom left, he made the choice to stay here and finish school. And he was the only one of the three guys [in Green Day] who would. Billie Joe didn't have a huge amount of support either, but Mike really didn't have anything. He was just self-motivated."

Isocracy (named after a state of government where everyone shares equal power) were punk enough for Gilman. Their notorious sets would often culminate with the band showering the audience with garbage they lugged over from the nearby dump. Isocracy's drummer, John Kiffmeyer, was four years older than the persistent teenagers from Rodeo. He was lean and handsome, while Mike was gangly and Billie still had baby fat. "I had a huge crush on him," Anna Armstrong Humann confessed. Sweet Children already worshipped the bands they saw every weekend, but bolstered by some weed, they invited Kiffmeyer to play with them one night in Pinole.

"John was going out with Eggplant's sister," remembers Sean Hughes. "I knew him because he came over our house one night and ate a bunch of the frozen dinners we'd been saving. So a month later me and Mike and Billie were walking through Pinole and this guy in an army jacket rides up on his motorcycle. He's still wearing the helmet and he asked us, 'Hey you guys ever been to Gilman Street? You ever heard of a band called Isocracy?' And I said, 'Yeah, one of those guys ate my frozen dinners!' And he said, 'What did he look like?' And I said, 'He was wearing a blue bandana?' And the guy pulled off his helmet and he was wearing a blue bandana. He said, 'You mean like this?'" As inauspicious as this Bugs Bunny–worthy scenario seemed, it would mark some serious changes in Sweet Children, setting them on their path to becoming a professional touring and recording act. "John was a goof, but he had a real serious side to him too," Hughes says. "He became kind of like our management."

Kiffmeyer's stage name was Al Sobrante, a winking alteration of El Sobrante, the suburban town where he lived, as had Pritchard and his mother. Nobody called him John. At Gilman, and everywhere else really, he was "Al."

"I met Al in fuckin' soccer camp, when I was like nine or ten or something," remembers Jeff Ott of Crimpshrine. "I was a weird kid, but when I met him I was like 'whoa, this kid's really weird.' He was just super intense about trivial, unimportant or bizarre things or just whatever. He was just like really overly enthusiastic about anything he was talking about all the time. And he was just kind of odd in that way. Really eccentric."

From the moment he joined, the high-strung, fast-talking Kiffmeyer considered himself to be the band's leader and used his age and hard-core credibility as a means of asserting his control. "Al's was a very type-A personality," recalls Patrick Hynes, a future employee at Lookout Records, although he was just nineteen years old. "He had to be in charge."

Kiffmeyer, it should probably be noted, was contacted several times with interview proposals for this book and declined to participate—at least we assume so since he didn't answer any of the e-mails we sent. For what it's worth, Green Day doesn't discuss him either.

"John deserves a lot of credit for getting [Sweet Children] out of the garage," current road manager Bill Schneider (then a member of Gilman punks Monsula) stresses. "Isocracy had been a very popular band. Their shows at Gilman would sell out, and they'd be the best party you could go to. They were already a really big band at the time but I think John knew, 'Wow these guys have something.'"

Still, Kiffmeyer's personality caused friction between the two unlikely matched parties. Armstrong, who considered himself the band's leader, let it slide at first since Kiffmeyer's membership nearly guaranteed them that coveted Gilman slot. Without him, Sweet Children were considered overly soft and young. With Kiffmeyer behind the drum kit, they became an interesting amalgam, with Isocracy's built-in fan base.

"That's when I first heard of them," says Christopher Appelgren, the current president of Lookout Records (and, at the time, sixteen-year-old Gilman-er). "There was a certain kind of social hierarchy, and all these people were really young in the Berkeley Gilman scene. John took Sweet Children from being these kinds of kids who maybe sort of hung out at Gilman the same way a lot of us did to actually being a real part of the scene."

Kiffmeyer influenced Billie Joe and Mike more in terms of punk ethics than musicality, which was natural at this point for the pair. He taught them to be fair and up front and brutally honest in their business dealings. Sweet Children would draw up a Xeroxed contract that they would send to people before shows. This was virtually unheard of on the local, small-time punk scene at the time. "It was a 'this is not a contract contract,'" Appelgren says, clarifying. "When they'd tour they'd be prepared. 'This is what we would like, if you have any food or beer, or if you can help us out with a place to stay, that would be great. We're asking for, but not requesting, at least $100.' Once they started playing, it was John who showed them how to deal with stuff like that. He played the dad role a little bit."

Sweet Children finally got their shot and landed at the bottom of a Gilman bill headlined by a bigger local act named Neurosis over the Thanksgiving holiday of 1988. Armstrong, Pritchard, and Kiffmeyer played a warm-up show at the restaurant where Billie Joe's mother worked, Rod's Hickory Pit—attended mostly by Armstrong's morally supportive family.

"It was definitely more of a family thing," David Armstrong recalls. "But the crowd was big. My mom had thirteen brothers and sisters. There were maybe a handful of punks there."

Their Gilman set was short and fast: a selection of originals, including "Sweet Children," "Strangeland," and "The Best Thing in Town," and covers like "Johnny B. Goode" and The Who's "My Generation." The gravity of the moment got the better of Armstrong that night. He was all but mum throughout the set. Fortunately, Kiffmeyer provided shtick *and* drum fills.

"I was at Sweet Children's very first Gilman show," Portman recalls. "And I thought their drummer talked too much. Giving the drummer a mic is never a good idea. I remember thinking they were good. They were a garage band, but they clearly had one thing [that set them apart from] a lot of punk bands: They could actually play their instruments. That was certainly rare in my experience. They were schlumpy, kind of dressed down, almost hippie kids. Scruffy, unkempt kids, but they had their act together."

"Compared with a lot of bands, they sort of made an instant name for themselves because everyone was surprised by how young they were. And because their music was on the polished side. They sang harmony, which was totally unusual," Jeff Ott says.

Sergie Loobkoff of Samiam, yet another beloved Berkeley cult act, tends to agree with Portman and Ott's descriptions. "I thought they sounded like REO Speedwagon," he says, laughing.

The Gilman set was well received and led to various house party slots. Armstrong, encouraged by the reaction to their first real gig, focused 100 percent of his energies on the band. He informed his mom that he would not be completing his senior year of high school. Pritchard remained enrolled. Armstrong was one day shy of eighteen. By the following morning, he'd no longer be a minor. The decision was all his. "I'm sort of a self-educated person," Armstrong says. "The only thing I really wanted to do was live up to our potential, and that was it.

We suddenly had this band that musically became pretty powerful, and we made a big noise. We just wanted to see where it could take us."

It's not that Armstrong was lazy, but there was a certain disconnect between working to make money and working for the sake of a band that could one day make him a lot of money. It seemed like a no-brainer to him. To his family and certain friends it seemed somewhat eccentric. Nobody was in doubt of his talent, but in Rodeo, everybody worked somewhere.

"Mike always wanted to make sure he paid his own way," David Armstrong says, and laughs. "Billie could give a shit. He was the baby. But Mike understood early. He made sure he graduated too. One night I was picking him up from guitar practice in my mom's station wagon. He was saying, 'I don't know about this.' It wasn't a big band breakup talk. The thing with Mike is that he's a worrier. And I think we was looking at it like 'Man, it's tough being a musician.' He wanted a fallback. Mike grew up faster than Billie, and he wanted to make sure he wasn't left out in the cold. But he stuck with it." Billie Joe, on the other hand, had no fallback. He'd muse aloud about how if it didn't work out, he'd become a pool cleaner, but it was clear, especially after the encouragement from admirers like Erica Paleno and John Kiffmeyer, that Sweet Children, in his mind at least, were going to work out. "Billie wasn't going to be happy doing anything else," David says.

"At that age, Billie was so into music that he was distracted by the rest of his life—the rest of his life was a distraction from him doing his music," Bill Schneider agrees. "He didn't have jobs—he was so content to sleep on somebody's couch. He just waited for Mike to get a place to live and then go sleep on the couch there. He was just distracted with having to live an ordinary life.

When necessary, Billie could choose from a number of punk rock crash pads. Many of them, however, were in dangerous parts of the city. "I would stay with him sometimes in these warehouses full of crusty punks," Paleno says. Small and slight, Armstrong walked the dark, broken glass–covered street with one eye perpetually fixed over his shoulder. Although terrifying, these stays were usually temporary, and one of them (at a particularly unsavory warehouse space, above a West Oakland brothel) inspired him to write what became one of Green Day's best-loved early songs, "Welcome to Paradise," which appears on both *Kerplunk!* and *Dookie,* in a rerecorded version. Armstrong learned in his preteens how to write himself out of a bad situation and continued to do so as he approached his early twenties. Any number of bad situations could equal a great song; and if that was the case, how bad could they really be?

> *Dear mother,*
> *Can you hear me whining?*
> *It's been three whole weeks*
> *since that I have left your home*
> *This sudden fear has left me trembling*
> *cause now it seems that I am out here on my own*
> *And I'm feeling so alone*
>
> *Pay attention to the cracked streets*
> *and the broken homes*
> *Some call it the slums*
> *some call it nice*
> *I want to take you through*
> *a wasteland I like to call*
> *my home*
> *Welcome to Paradise*
> —lyrics reprinted by permission

Even as late as 1992, when he had two indie releases under his belt, Armstrong was essentially an extremely talented homeless kid. "I'm not living anywhere," he told *Flipside* that year. "I have my stuff at my mom's house. I drive around and hang out with my friends and kind of end up where I end up that night. I don't live on the street. I hang out. I have places to go."

No matter where he was sleeping, Armstrong would always make it to band rehearsals or shows on time, even when he had no money for the transit fare or gas for the '77 Datsun he'd purchased and nicknamed "Thor." Although Mike had grown much more successful at balancing the band with a necessary paying job and school, he was in many ways still as troubled as he was in his early youth. He would have had to bottle up his feelings had Armstrong, and their music, not been such a constant presence, helping him to process them.

"I think we're the first ones to yell at each other," Mike has said, "but we're also the first ones to be there when the other's life is totally falling apart." Mike had good reason to focus on the band in addition to the practicalities (working, studying) which always threatened to distract him. Sweet Children, who were at first beyond the pale, were developing a surprisingly large following at 924 Gilman Street as well as on the house party circuit. Six months earlier, they were the kiddie band. Now, on the basis of their live set as much as Kiffmeyer's local cred, they were a bona fide draw.

They were also a trio. The addition of a real drummer was, perhaps, a factor in Sean Hughes deciding that playing in a band was not his forte. "I left and Mike switched to bass," he recalls. "He was definitely more talented than I was. I wasn't trying that hard. I took lessons, but I never practiced. They were gunning to switch up anyway, and I just dropped out. By then, they were really organized. They were definitely cruising." Mike learned the rudimentary details of bass playing in even less time than it took him to learn rhythm guitar. He'd carry his bass case with him to school and spend lunch hours and breaks plucking the heavy strings. Unamplified, the instrument emitted a sound soon to be familiar to many of his friends and Pinole High classmates: *Dirnt . . . dirnt, dirnt, dirnt, dirnt.* The noise was so prevalent that Michael Pritchard soon became jokingly referred to as Mike Dirnt. In classic punk-rock fashion, he took what might have been a slight (albeit an affectionate one) and turned it into something proud. From then on he was (and for the duration of this biography, we will refer to him as) Mike Dirnt, bassist extraordinaire.

In Northern (as in Southern) California, house parties were almost constant in the Oakland and Berkeley suburbs and a vital source of exposure, food, beer, and cash for young bands. Keggers with kids kept many of them alive long enough to sign with indies and record. "House parties were important to the scene. They were everywhere. NOFX, in 1986, did an all house-party U.S. tour. Mostly they were like two dollars to get in, and there would be a keg, and we'd end up with fifty bucks a night, and it was perfect," Fat Mike says. "I saw Sweet Children at a backyard party in Berkeley, probably 1989," Fat Mike recalls. "There were probably forty people there, and one of them was standing about four feet in front of Billie and spit right in his face. And Billie just kept playing! He didn't even wipe it till the song was over. I always thought that was crazy. I hate getting spit on. I guess he was trying to be punk."

"For every show you played at a real club you played five parties," Schneider says. "Everybody just had parties so the bands could play. And you all toured [house parties] at the same time. We'd go around the country, and there was a real strong network—it was a really interesting time because there was a lot of young people into music so we could travel around the country and we could play in people's backyards and basements and at vet's halls. We'd still make enough money every night from selling T-shirts, demo tapes, and maybe we'd get paid eighty bucks from the door and we could go on tour for a few months. It was even easier after getting signed to an indie. Having 7-inch singles out that people could buy kind of almost made you a rock star in that world."

It was at one of these house parties that Armstrong, Dirnt, and Kiffmeyer first caught the attention of Lawrence Livermore, then thirty-two and a former hippie turned mountain-dwelling punk entrepreneur. As he would with several key Gilman acts, Livermore would prove to be Sweet Children's first and most important supporter: a friend and a label boss.

Like Tim Yohannan, Livermore was too old to pass for a Generation Xer but still too vivid, angry, and ambitious to cede to yuppiedom as most of his peers. He still related to the youth mentality. "I'd always tended to look and act younger than my actual age," Livermore says today. "That might be a nice way of saying that I was immature. If anything, though, I'd say it was an asset; having already been through one countercultural experience with the hippies, I'd had a chance to learn from the mistakes and excesses people are prone to when they get caught up in what seem to be vital social movements."

Lookout, the Xeroxed 'zine that Livermore began circulating in the late eighties, had little to do with punk rock. At first, it was merely a newsletter for the community of Northern Californian oddballs who'd retreated from the city for one reason or another and took to the mountains to homestead it. "[The magazine] was for misfits, pot growers, and back-to-the-landers in a remote area of Northern Mendocino County," Livermore remembers. "It was actually the pot growers who helped drive me into turning it into a punk rock 'zine. They threatened to burn my house down if I didn't stop writing about local stuff."

Unlike *MRR* or *Search and Destroy, Lookout* had an air of a manifesto about it, with subjective rants about the environment and politics. Livermore was, after all, its sole contributor (call it a proto-punk blog). "My punk rock readers in the

Bay Area probably saw *Lookout* as more iconoclastic than the standard punk 'zines," he theorized. "That probably gave me a credibility that the others lacked, so when I started writing about East Bay bands and the Gilman scene, I think they took it as more than just ordinary hype and attached a lot more importance to the developing scene than they might have otherwise."

Lookout Records, which grew out of the 'zine's unlikely popularity, was initially just a venture designed to release an album by The Lookouts, Livermore's punk band, which featured a drum prodigy from nearby Willits, California, named Frank Edwin Wright. Born December 9, 1972, Wright was only twelve years old when he first became a punk drummer. By seventeen, he would replace John Kiffmeyer and help lead Green Day into history. At the time, however, he was studying clowning with tie-dyed icon Wavy Gravy and banging on pots and pans with sticks.

"Nobody called him Frank," says Cathy Livingston, Tre Wright's schoolteacher. "Willits is a little town not far from my ranch," Winston Smith says. "There's no electricity, no running water. Just kerosene lamps. Tre definitely grew up in that situation."

Tre's father, Frank Wright II, had served as a helicopter pilot in Vietnam. When he returned home from duty, he relocated his wife, Linda, daughter Lori, and young son to the mountains of Mendocino. Like Billie Joe's father, Frank Wright II drove trucks for a living and, like most people in the mountains of Mendocino, he had rumored ties to the Grateful Dead (who on occasion were ostensibly the cargo in one of Mr. Wright's rigs).

Wright often noticed his son banging on rocks, tree trunks, rusting bicycles.

"I thumped things," Tre Cool recalls today with typical wit and brevity. As a child he was hyperintelligent and the bashing of inanimate objects was more likely the product of an overactive and understimulated brain. "Tre's family lived sort of off the grid up above Laytonville," Cathy Livingston says, "and so did we for a while. Up in the mountains. No power, no phone. You had to make that yourself."

Tre's penchant for acting out and the humor that results from his dark side are likely because he was exposed to his father's postwar mentality at such a young age. "His dad was a helicopter pilot in Vietnam and had some pretty hard-core experiences and definitely has scars, mental scars, from it still to this day," Bill Schneider says. Happily, by the time he was twelve, whenever Frank would have his dark moments (he was by all accounts easy-going otherwise), Tre would retreat to a neighbor's house, where he would play on a vacated drum kit. Like Billie Joe with his guitar and Mike with his bass, mastering the drums made Tre feel capable and safe.

"What do you do if your kid can only count to four?" Cool joked to *Flipside* in 1992. "Buy him a drum kit and call him gifted." It was a good drummer joke, as far as bad drummer jokes go; but Livermore saw that Tre had genuine musical talent and labored to place his manic energy in some practical context. Livermore's girlfriend, Anne, had recently left him and, up until that point, had been the drummer in his fantasy band. Eager to replace her and keep the band going, Livermore didn't see Tre's age as a liability. His behavior was a different story. "He was loud, obnoxious, ebullient, unruly, and hyperactive. At the same time, he had an undeniable charm that enabled him to get away with what might be considered unbearably bratty behavior," he recalls. "It sometimes took a certain amount of patience to deal with him, but for the most part it was a real joy working with him. He was so enthusiastic about learning to play music."

Another local kid, a fourteen-year-old homesteader named

Kain was recruited to play bass, even though he lacked Tre's natural ability and rhythm. Although it may seem suspicious today, at the time, it didn't seem odd that a grown man was spending so much time with the neighborhood kids. "I wouldn't say that Larry was a mentor," says Wendy Norris, another childhood friend. "I just think that because he had a youthful spirit, [Tre] and everyone else was really comfortable about it. It wasn't like he was this lonely old guy who hung around with little boys."

Happily, nobody in Willits complained of the noise, and young Tre could bash away at his kit at all hours. People in Willits and neighboring Laytonville minded their own business anyway. "Half the town was loggers, ranchers, and truckers," says Zan Cannon, a classmate of Tre's. "And the other half was hippies, growing things and smoking things and living barefoot. There was a lot of marijuana consumption. Not down in town. But I mean, everybody knew what was going on up in the hills."

"All you do is get fucked up," Cool confirmed in a 1994 interview in *Spin*. "There's nothing else to do. It's like 'What'd you do yesterday?' 'Smoked a fatty and drank a six-pack.'"

"The band jelled really quickly," Livermore says of the Lookouts' early practices. "I wanted to call us the Lookouts because of the magazine, which was, in turn, named after the fire lookout tower that was one of the most visible landmarks in our canyon; by then it had achieved considerable notoriety, and I thought it would be an asset to the band to have an immediately recognizable name." Livermore was genuinely ambitious and would be quick to tell any of the locals that the band was a serious enterprise, not some novelty act or weekend hobby. This was vital punk rock for all involved.

"It was a little funny," Wendy Norris says. "Punk rock just wasn't big up there. I think that was more of an urban thing.

People up there were listening to the Grateful Dead. You know, mellow stuff."

"I didn't treat him like a little kid unless he was acting like one, and as time went on, that happened less and less often," Livermore says, recounting Tre's slow but sure progression toward serious and disciplined musicianship. The Lookouts, like Sweet Children, practiced long and often. "By the time he was fourteen, he was a highly skilled drummer and performer and very mature in his own loud, obnoxious, ebullient, unruly, hyperactive way."

The Lookouts performed one of their first performances "off the mountain," as the locals say, at Grapevine Station, a gas station/general store off Highway 101 with an outdoor picnic area. Not many saw this historic event, but those who did were forever changed. "I remember them playing a song called 'Fuck Religion,'" Norris says. "And we were all laughing because Tre was singing and his voice hadn't changed yet. He was really young. And so he had like this little Judy Garland voice, singing 'Fuck religion! Preachers are whores!'"

Livermore is the one who christened Wright "Tre Cool," shortly into his tenure with the band. With his new moniker and an integral role in Willits's only multigenerational punk combo, it wasn't long before Tre started looking beyond the mountaintop. He took his equivalency exams, got his GED, and left high school early.

Tre's parents knew that if he was going to make it, he would need to leave Willits. They knew he was special, so they supported his decision. "Everybody knew he wanted to be a drummer," Cannon says. "That day he was going to head down to the Bay Area." "He talked about his band and cut this record and sold me a tape for four bucks. I still have that," remembers Livingston. "I understand that at the high-school level he lost interest. And probably properly so. He had other things to do." By sixteen, Tre Cool was already a regular on the

Gilman scene, sitting in with bands, attending parties, and gaining notoriety for his unruly sense of humor, serious drum skills, and youth.

"I don't want to say everybody hated them, OK? I don't want to say that at all," Jeff Ott says. "But people didn't take the Lookouts seriously because Lawrence was older than us, or something like that. At the time Tre was just an anomaly. He was the little kid in the Lookouts."

Tre knew Billie Joe Armstrong and Mike Dirnt. He understood that they were in a band; but perhaps because he was self-conscious about their ages, he never really socialized with them. If they did find themselves in the same crowd, they exchanged friendly nods of acknowledgment. None of them could have guessed the effect they would soon have on one another's lives.

Chapter Four

OP IVY

Lawrence Livermore didn't start a label to gain respect for his occasionally maligned punk band, but that's what happened nonetheless. Livermore was so inspired by the bands he'd see at Gilman that, after a while, both the 'zine and the band took a backseat to the daily operation of the indie label he co-founded with David Hayes, who would leave to form his own label a few years later. Livermore and Hayes called the label Lookout—same as the 'zine and the band—and it became a ticket to the world for Green Day and their fellow Gilman Street punk bands. It would not be Green Day, however, who would put Lookout on the map.

Without Operation Ivy, a short-lived but brilliant ska punk quartet, there may not have even been a Green Day. Op Ivy, made up of guitarist Tim Armstrong (who used to go by the punk name "Lint"), drummer Dave Mello, bassist Matt Freeman, and singer Jesse Michaels, became Billie Joe Armstrong's favorite band and biggest influence. Musically, Op Ivy were tight and raw at the same time; aesthetically, they looked great and had iconic graphics and cool clothes; and politically, they were activists but didn't preach. It was enlightened music, but it was also fun.

"Everyone's got their band," Billie Joe Armstrong said

during our 2005 *Spin* interview, "and I've got to say Operation Ivy was definitely one that changed me. And it's a proven fact that music can change people."

Armstrong found Op Ivy at the right time, just as his own band was beginning to feel their own power and draw crowds. Op Ivy was slightly older than Sweet Children, but it didn't matter. Op Ivy exploded onto 924 Gilman Street fully formed, and they drilled into Billie Joe's head that a local band could accomplish a lot, go very far, and move people a great deal.

"Operation Ivy was one of the bands that quite literally formed in and around Gilman," Livermore says. "One day [Tim] came running up to me saying, 'Larry, I'm in a new band. We're called Operation Ivy, and we're playing tonight!' So I watched them, and before they'd finished their first song, I decided I wanted to do a record with them. I think they were a little shocked but that's how I made most of my decisions to sign bands. I'd just see them, be excited, and spontaneously ask them to do a record. Half the time I didn't even know I was going to ask them until I'd already done so. Screeching Weasel came out to California from Chicago and played a gig with Operation Ivy—that's how I ended up doing their records. In turn, I got to work with the Queers because Screeching Weasel singer Ben Weasel kept bugging me to listen to their demo. I listened, I loved it, and the next thing I knew, we had yet another great band."

Just as with Billie Joe and Mike Dirnt, Op Ivy's core members had known one another since they were kids and, therefore, shared a similarly intense bond. "I first met Jesse in early 1983," Tim Armstrong says. "He was thirteen and was playing in a band with Jeff Ott. Jeff was twelve at the time. I would see Jesse hanging around Telegraph Avenue. We played video games a few times together at Universal Records and liked each other. Then one day he just split town. The rumors were that he went to live with his mom in Pittsburgh. Then out of nowhere I started to see him hanging out again. It was one of those cold, gray East Bay afternoons in February 1987. We were hanging out at the downtown BART station in Berkeley with nothing to do. I told him that me and Matt Freeman were starting a band. We had the same influences and listened to the same records. Stiff Little Fingers, Social Unrest, the Specials, Bad Manners, and Discharge, to name a few."

Op Ivy played their first show at drummer Dave Mello's parents' house in nearby Albany, California, in April 1987. The following night, they made their debut at Gilman Street and were instantly the talk of the scene. The difference may have been simple personal chemistry: the energy and interaction among the members onstage. Whatever it was, Op Ivy were close to being an overnight success like none Gilman Street had ever seen before.

"Me and Tim used to fight a lot," Michaels acknowledges, "but we were a really good team in terms of creating music. I don't know how the chemistry works, but it seems like something about the fighting was a part of it. We wrote better stuff than I've been able to write since then. So I think we had a really good group even though sometimes we couldn't stand one another. It was a fortuitous gathering of the right people."

"Operation Ivy was everything you really wanted," recalls David Katznelson. "You know, it was that wonderful side of reggae ska mixed with pop and punk; it was killer. And they played everywhere." Sweet Children marveled not only at Op Ivy's ability to destroy a crowd but also at the band's reach. Throughout their two-year existence, Operation Ivy was one of the few Gilman Street bands that made it to the East Coast: They played in New Jersey, Pennsylvania, and Connecticut.

"We'd travel to play anywhere," Michaels says, "like community centers. It was just constantly going on here, so the thing to do was to get in a band, hopefully a decent band, although it almost didn't matter, and then play these shows. It was just the raddest thing in the world. We played one show in a barn."

"It was in Hillsburg, California," Tim Armstrong confirms. "We played in front of a handful of punks and farm animals." Op Ivy not only toured, but also recorded, and sounded great. Their first released recordings, "Officer" and "I Got No," appeared on the 1987 Maximumrocknroll compilation EP *Turn It Around* (along with tracks by Isocracy, Sewer Trout, Soup, No Use for a Name, Corrupted Morals, Stikky, Nasal Sex, and the all-female rap parody act Yeastie Girls).

Despite their success, Op Ivy weren't making much money. "Our first tour, in 1988, paid seventy-five dollars," Tim Armstrong recalls. "The only time we received more than that was after playing with Fugazi and Verbal Assault at the Rocket in Providence. And that was because Ian [MacKaye, Fugazi's leader] split the band's money with us. We got a hundred and fifty dollars."

Still, from the other side of the stage, it was easy for smaller bands to believe that Operation Ivy made it, and for them to make it too they had to get in the van. They needed a record deal. They needed everything Op Ivy had. And they needed to be that good.

There were some punks who resented the band's skyrocketing popularity. Dismissive cries of "ska boy" or "pretty boy" could be heard between their sets. "They were a little more cute," Gina Arnold explains. For the most part, however, they were beloved: the scene's first organic phenomenon. "We were humanistic," Michaels says. "At the end of every show we would grab people from the audience and just put them onstage until the stage was really mobbed up with people. It was mainly just for fun and a good set closer, but it was also about the whole thing being a big party and not a rock-star thing."

It was too good to last. And it didn't. Many people widely

blame external pressure for Op Ivy's premature end midway through 1989.

Armstrong famously provided an official eulogy for his old band in the song "Journey to the End of the East Bay." It appears on . . . *And Out Come the Wolves*, the 1995 release from his more popular and long-running, but less influential, post–Operation Ivy project, Rancid. "Too much attention," he explains in the song, "unavoidably destroyed us."

Sweet Baby Jesus, the scene's less popular ska-punk band, had signed a deal with Slash Records, which was distributed by major label Warner Brothers. Everyone was looking to Op Ivy to do the same, although it wasn't necessarily an option then, as far as Michaels remembers. "Major labels back then, they were just not interested in punk. Pre-Nirvana and pre–Green Day. It was kind of a different world. I think the whole time we played, I honestly don't think we talked to more than two or three label people; and if we did, they were probably pretending to be more interested than they actually were. Now when a band plays they're talking about, 'Well should we shoot for Warner Brothers or Reprise?' At that time, without any value judgment, you could've been playing for five years and never had a single conversation like that. You'd just go, 'This rules!' Not, 'Well, we've made it.'"

"There's always a beginning and an end to everything," Tim Armstrong says. "We had just run our course. We were a band for exactly two years, twenty-four months. Like putting flame to gasoline, Operation Ivy burned bright from its inception. We just stopped before it dimmed."

"They broke up way too soon," Billie Joe lamented in the 2005 *Spin* interview, but as far as the preservation of a near-perfect band myth, Op Ivy broke up at just the right time. Their Lookout single and full-length releases are considered classics of the modern rock era—musts for every college record collection or indie bar jukebox.

"Operation Ivy would have been huge if they'd stuck

around," Lawrence Livermore theorizes. "They've sold well over half a million records without even being around— pretty remarkable for a band that broke up the same month their first and only album came out. But I don't know how long they would have lasted in any event; the chemistry within the band was probably too volatile for that."

It was rumored that Michaels dropped out of modern society to become a Buddhist monk. This is not entirely false but somewhat exaggerated. "I was kind of falling away from it all. Didn't go to Gilman as much," he says. "I went away for a year and studied Buddhism at local Zen centers. A lot of Green Day's ascension happened while I was away. I missed a lot of it. I was pretty surprised."

Tim Armstrong began a long bender in the wake of Op Ivy. "It got really bad. I almost died a few times. In 1991, my brother found me on Telegraph Avenue really fucked up. He dragged me into his car, where I passed out. He took me to the hospital; I had a .39 blood alcohol level, which kinda scared my family. It took me four years to make another record." By the time Rancid's self-titled 1993 debut (on indie label Epitaph) was released, the world would be ready for Armstrong, his disciples, and punk rock in general. The world changed, but it was bands like Op Ivy on the West Coast, and Fugazi on the East, who paved the way for it all.

"You could say that when Op Ivy went away, Green Day became the biggest band on the scene," Jeff Ott theorizes. Tellingly, Green Day supported Operation Ivy on their final Gilman show. That night, May 28, 1989, was also Green Day's debut as Green Day. Sweet Children had grown up, and a new and more powerful incarnation was about to take over.

Chapter Five

HUGE IN PETALUMA

The surprise success of Operation Ivy's 7-inch single "Hectic," which was released in January 1988, brought unforeseen funds into Lookout Records and gave Livermore confidence and momentum. Still, he wasn't expecting very much from Sweet Children when he signed them to a modest record deal.

"They played a show with the Lookouts that only five kids turned up for," Livermore says. "They played by candlelight, too, because it was in a mountain cabin with only a generator for power. But, as I've often said, they played for those five kids as if they were The Beatles at Shea Stadium, and just as with Op Ivy, I knew before they finished their first song that I wanted to do their record. They were way more pop than the other Gilman bands—too pop, I thought, to have much of a chance at doing well on that scene. But I thought the songs and the performances were so good that they deserved to be captured on vinyl, even if I did end up losing a little money on it."

Livermore could not have guessed that as Sweet Children prepared to record their first EP for Lookout, *39/Smooth*, it would be a band called Green Day that would deliver the record. To this day, the band tends to agree with people who think their band name is goofy. In an interview that took place in a New Orleans hotel room in the late fall of 2004, they seemed grateful that Hoobastank had a big hit that year. "At last a band with a worse name than us," Mike Dirnt said joking.

The record deal prompted the band to visualize their name on a CD or a vinyl EP, and "Sweet Children" seemed to remind everyone just how much of a baby band they still were. Green Day was a signal to all on the scene that they were older. And very, very stoned. As with Sweet Children, the name "Green Day" also comes from a Billie Joe Armstrong original. The song is a slice of after-school special, gateway drug rock about the discovery of an alternate dimension via smoking out in your bedroom.

A small cloud has fallen
the white mist hits the ground
My lungs comfort me with joy
verging on one detail
The rest just crowds around
My eyes itch of burning red

Picture sounds
of moving insects so surreal
lay around
Looks like I found something new
    —lyrics reprinted by permission

"I think the general feeling was that the first name wasn't a very good choice, and that the second one was better," Jeff Ott says. "Plus, they were total potheads."

The remarkable thing about listening to the pair of EPs that Green Day recorded for Lookout—"1,000 Hours" in 1989 and "Slappy" in 1990—is how ready the band sounds. It would be years before their songs were mixed up to arena-worthy power but even without the 20/20 hindsight, you can tell that this is a band that, at its best, was not afraid to get there. A strong sense of internal quality control made sure every song was fully formed.

"I give 100 percent [commitment] to a song [while I'm writing it]," Armstrong says, describing his process, "even if it's 100 percent a piece of shit." Fortunately, writing the latter seldom happens. Like Ray Davies before him, Billie Joe has a gift for mass-producing tunes that are similar yet distinctive enough to amount to a real style. Each one is vaguely melancholy, but they take on a spirited toughness when worked up with the band—his sounding board throughout the years. It's as if he is a sensitive singer-songwriter at heart but somehow fell in with the punks and remained there. "I never purposely write sad songs," he says. "It's just something that naturally comes out. The way we do it, it becomes sad and uplifting at the same time."

Unlike most singer-songwriters, however, Armstrong is a giver. He writes to reach others as well as to express himself. This is another reason why Green Day has enjoyed such loyalty among their fan base throughout the years. As a lyricist, he is inclusive and unpretentious. "Good lyrics have always been important to me," he says. "Once somebody gets it, it's like 'Oh that's cool.'"

During the 1989 Christmas holiday, when studio time was cheap, Armstrong, Dirnt, and Kiffmeyer recorded their full-length debut for Lookout: *39/Smooth* at Berkeley's Art of Ears studios. With *39/Smooth*, the song craft takes yet another step forward, especially the lyrics. Although only eighteen, Armstrong delivers a striking, reflective track reminiscent of The Beatles' "In My Life." Amid the frenetic punk of "At the Library" and "The Judge's Daughter," "I Was There" foreshadows the introspective sensibility that would later set Green Day apart from other successful punk bands, and give us sensitive hits such as "Good Riddance (Time of Your Life)," "Waiting," and most recently "Wake Me Up When September Ends."

Looking back upon my life
and the places that I've been
Pictures, faces, girls I've loved
I try to remember when
Faded memories on the wall
some names I have forgotten
But each one is a memory I
look back on so often.

I look into the past
I want to make it last
I was there

I look into the past
I want to make it last
I was there

Looking back what I have done
there's lots more life to live
At times I feel overwhelmed
I question what I can give
But I don't let it get me down
or cause me too much sorrow
There's no doubt about who I am
I always have tomorrow.

　　　　—lyrics reprinted by permission

In fewer than five years, they'd be banned from the scene, but by 1990, Green Day's full-length debut *39/Smooth* received acclaim both locally and, with Lookout's ever-increasing reach, nationally. "Some of the bands that were coming through my studio were rocking it on a cassette and saying, 'Check this out, man. Have you heard Green Day? They're really good!'" remembers Brett Gurewitz. "You know I liked how it was a little more pop, and it had like a sixties vibe."

Green Day played dozens of Gilman shows, many of them benefit concerts for the label or local fanzines such as *Cometbus,* run by scenester/musician Aaron Cometbus (who would play in Armstrong's side project Pinhead Gunpowder). But Green Day's local popularity wasn't enough to satisfy them. In June of 1990, they mounted their first van tour that year in support of the debut.

They left the day Mike graduated from Pinole High. "Billie and John were waiting for him on the street," David Armstrong recalls. Billie Joe had purchased his older brother Allen's orange Ford Econoline 150 van. The band gutted the back and outfitted it with lofts for storing their gear and sleeping. Sean Hughes joined them as de facto roadie. "We just loaded in our shit and took off," he says with a laugh.

With Sobrante driving, the band hit forty-five stops along the way, from bars to house parties to small punk clubs across the country.

"The tour was awesome," Hughes recalls. "We all got out of Rodeo, which we had all talked about: 'Man, I wanna do something. I wanna go somewhere besides here.' We'd hung out in Berkeley, but we'd never seen the country. We were totally on our own. We didn't have much money. The itinerary was set up through John, and we just headed out."

At each tour stop, Green Day would encounter crowds of varying size, full of juvenile skate rats, indie-minded college kids, wastoids, and preppies looking to get blitzed and hear something loud. "Different cities, different states, different scenes," Hughes recalls. "And we just passed through. We weren't old enough to drink, so most of the shows were on college campuses."

During a sparsely attended show in Minneapolis in 1990, Billie Joe, then eighteen, met an attractive twenty-two-year-old woman with brown eyes, olive skin, and dark hair that she wore in dreadlocks. Adrienne Nesser was enrolled at University of Minnesota, where she studied sociology.

Armstrong had never met anyone like Adrienne, even among the politically correct and progressive Gilman Street scene, which, truth be told, was largely boy-dominated. Although he was a high school dropout, Nesser didn't make him feel intellectually intimidated. She was a punk rocker, after all, partial to hair dye and thrift store dresses. He was a punk. They had a bond and an instant attraction.

Unlike most stops, Minneapolis had a thriving indie rock scene, and the band was able to park the van and stay a bit longer than usual. Kiffmeyer was able to line up more than one gig. "We got to relax a little bit," Hughes says. "We had a longer break." Adrienne had a boyfriend (also named Billy, oddly enough) and Armstrong was still dating Paleno, so the pair did nothing but talk on that first trip but sometimes, given the right chemistry, conversation is plenty. When the band packed up the Econoline and headed east (they'd reach as far as Rhode Island and eventually as far south as Florida before returning to Berkeley), Adrienne's face, voice, clothes, and smell were firmly rooted in the teenager's consciousness. They exchanged phone numbers, and Billie Joe made a point to call her at various tour stops when he was feeling especially chatty or lonely.

"I remember on the way back, he was trying to take a picture of a road sign that said 80," Sean Hughes recalls, "because he was thinking of Adrienne and he called her 'Aidy.'"

As exciting as the tour was, it wasn't without calamity and frustration.

"I saw Green Day on that first tour when they played Memphis," remembers Jason White, who would later play with Pinhead Gunpowder and Green Day on their last three major tours. "They got to the venue late, showed up when we were already loading out. The promoter had already given people half their money back. [On] those early tours, you create ridiculous goals for yourself because you don't know anything about traveling. You think, 'Well we're going from New Orleans to Little Rock, and yeah we have time to make it there if we leave by noon or something.' You just don't realize how long it takes to get anywhere really. You're a little green or whatever as far as touring goes."

Armstrong and Paleno broke up shortly after Green Day returned to Northern California, but it did little to calm his restlessness or quell any longing thoughts about his new Minneapolis non-girlfriend, to whom his mind kept returning. Home, alone, jobless, and conflicted, he'd sit in his room, smoke, and strum his guitar. Eventually, these feelings would be poured into a shimmering pop lament entitled "2,000 Light Years Away," which is about missing a girl he barely knew but suspected he didn't want to live without. It would become a mix tape favorite, embraced by dozens of young lovers separated by miles of road. Nesser continued to be Armstrong's muse for the duration of his career, inspiring love songs both oblique (like track "80," which was a winking take on his nickname for her) and direct (the 2000 track "Church on Sunday" is a harrowing account of a domestic rift).

In 1991, however, even with Paleno temporarily estranged (she'd continue to be a band supporter and friend), Nesser was not the songwriter's sole inspiration. It was around this time that Billie Joe began a relationship with another Gilman Street punk rocker named Amanda. A bit of an iron-willed feminist, Amanda's naturally rebellious character proved another great influence on Billie. He knew punk rock was supposed to be defiant, but he'd yet to be romantically involved with someone who embodied it. Paleno was too sweet and supportive. The original Maximum Rock and Roller females were a decade removed and many of them still considered Green Day eager children. Like Yohannan, Livermore, and Aaron Cometbus and, it seemed, any self-respecting, politically minded Bay Area punk, Amanda produced and distributed her own 'zine. She was fierce. She was also the first girl to dump him. "He got really into her, and she left him," Paleno says. "She didn't care about any of his success later, either. She bailed and joined the Peace Corps." His inability to impress or ensnare Amanda for long wounded Billie Joe. She is the subject of "Good Riddance (Time of Your Life)," one of Green Day's biggest hits, and one of the most misinterpreted pop songs of the last two decades (a bitter kiss-off, heard by most as a sweet love song). Whether or not Amanda was the mythical "one that got away" is not really important. What's interesting is that Armstrong has never stopped writing about her . . . or the idea of her. "She's a Rebel" on *American Idiot* is also based on her influence. She made him tougher by sharing her feisty views, and somehow older by breaking or at least scarring his heart. To paraphrase Billie Joe's beloved Replacements, color him sort of permanently impressed.

The debut tour was a personal and professional success, with the band enjoying enthusiastic crowds far from the familiar confines of 924 Gilman—it seemed, for a few weeks at least, as if it would be the band's last. John Kiffmeyer decided that he didn't really fancy a life of rest stops, crash pads, and haggling for their post-show fees. Kiffmeyer was planning to attend Humboldt State College in Arcata, California, in the fall.

Dirnt hadn't planned on attending college, and for high-school dropout Armstrong it wasn't even an option. While Kiffmeyer never actually informed them that he was leaving—and perhaps expected them to simply wait for him to join them on breaks—Armstrong and Dirnt realized that this was a serious threat to their hard-earned momentum. "Nobody was going to college," Jeff Ott observes. "Nobody was doing any particular work. All they really had was the band. They had to keep doing what they were doing."

Along with everyone else on the Gilman scene, Armstrong

knew that Tre Cool was one of the best local drummers. As it happened, he was available. "By 1990 the Lookouts were playing only occasionally, and we were living in separate cities," Livermore recounted. "We got together in July to record some new songs, and Billie Joe came along to play some lead guitar and sing backups. That was the first time he and Tre played together. Billie asked Tre to jam with him and Mike. They played their first show together in November, and it just sort of naturally evolved from there. John played a couple more shows with them that winter, but the band wanted to play all the time, and, to be quite blunt, Tre was quite simply a far better drummer."

Armstrong also knew that Cool was a handful. "Tre kind of had a bad reputation for being a real prankster and a real jokester," Paleno says. "And I remember Billie telling me, 'Well, he's a great drummer and we like him, but he's just one of those people you gotta keep an eye on because you never know what he's gonna say. Whether it's going to get you kicked out of a club or off a show.' But when Tre joined the band, *bam*— they just took off. They were that much better. He was the missing element. Plus John wasn't a pot smoker and Tre was, and that really was the Green Day common thread, the pot smoking."

"I thought we were the best band in the world," Cool said, describing the early sessions with Billie and Mike. Armstrong and Dirnt were amazed by Tre Cool's confidence. Kiffmeyer had retained his place in the band through a steady process of subtle derision. Cool didn't resort to power struggles because he was, at eighteen, content to kick ass and have fun. "Tre is the kind of person who walks through a party and fights will start behind him left and right," Dirnt once observed, describing his bandmate's anarchic energy. "And he'll walk out the back door with a girl on each arm and say, 'So where are we going next?' He's unscathed. Totally oblivious."

"He's a rock star," Armstrong agrees. "[He was] born a rock

star." "I think the biggest element Tre added in addition to being one of the best drummers in rock 'n' roll was the whole zany, crazy thing," says Chris Appelgren. "Billie and Mike always came across as a little more serious and quiet before Tre joined the band."

Cool's musicianship and spirit more than made up for his often erratic behavior and lack of an internal censor. "A few times Tre *did* say some things that were in poor taste," Appelgren says. "I remember asking Billie, 'Is this going to work?' And finally he told me, 'You know what? I love him. He's my brother now. He's in my band and he can do whatever he wants. We don't need to make excuses for him. He is who he is and he's here to stay.'"

With Tre Cool on board, Green Day were finally the Green Day we know today. It's another example of that weird rock chemistry: Take away one element, add another crucial element, and the whole mixture becomes highly combustible. "There are archetypes for this kind of thing," theorizes music historian Matt Pinfield. "Ringo replacing Pete Best. Dave Grohl replacing Chad Channing in Nirvana. There's always that kind of synergy that has to do with people involved in anything that makes it a success or lack of success. And it absolutely happened with Green Day." "When John was in the band," Chris Appelgren recalls, "it was like Mike and Billie and then there was John. With Tre, it was the three of them."

The only problem was that John Kiffmeyer still considered himself Green Day's drummer. "Tre was the official sanctioned 'temporary' drummer," Appelgren remembers. "That was the original idea; Tre was not a threat because he had been friends with everybody for a long time, and John being the taller, bigger guy was not easily intimidated. But then there was a show in Petaluma with Bad Religion, and I remember John knew about the show and came down expecting to play it. And Tre was there expecting to play it, too, and it was sort of this showdown. I wasn't at the show, but from what I understood, John did play. I think that experience of him wanting the band to exist at his convenience and on his terms made them realize they couldn't do that. They weren't at college, and they wanted to keep moving on. I think John thought, 'Well, this is my band. I'm gonna come down and play the show.' He played the show, but I think it was his last one because of how he did that. I think they felt bullied by it."

Armstrong had to struggle to assert his leadership over Kiffmeyer due to the latter's age and experience, but now Green Day had their first major tour behind them as well as their first record. Armstrong was eighteen going on nineteen. He studied and absorbed what he could use from Al Sobrante and moved along. This was, in many ways, a pattern for his ongoing informal education. "I think artistically and musically, Billie Joe was always the band's leader," Chris Appelgren observes. "And there was always a real understanding that the music came from him."

Kiffmeyer stuck around long enough to help with the production of Green Day's next Lookout full-length album *Kerplunk!* He would later play drums in local act the N'er Do Wells, but as Green Day went on to fame and fortune, Kiffmeyer slowly receded into civilian life, which is, by most accounts, quiet and happy. "He's married and has a family, a son, and a good life," Appelgren says. "He does some film production; I think he does lighting out of San Francisco. He was in another band that was on Lookout a while ago, and they moved on without him. He might have held a grudge for a time and his ego was bruised."

The DIY punk spirit Kiffmeyer helped imbue them with via his own influence and by virtually chaperoning them into the Gilman Street scene sticks with the band to this day. "What Green Day was ultimately able to do is take [punk] to new places," Appelgren continues. "It was not going to be just be a symbolic fuck you to the rest of the world and like, 'We're gonna stay in our small little clubhouse.' They were really going to take the spirit of the underdog and the misfit to a larger level in their own way. I think that to me is tremendous and something to be proud of and maybe John didn't have the vision to do that."

With Tre Cool in, Green Day also gained a sort of universal teen appeal that they lacked with Kiffmeyer. Cool, like Armstrong and Dirnt, *was* a teenager. The subsequent live dates brought an element to Gilman that hadn't really been seen there before: teenage girls. Punk rockers, with very few exceptions (such as Billy Idol and basically . . . Billy Idol), had not been crush worthy. Green Day embodied that "so homely they're adorable" appeal that has created unlikely heartthrobs from Frank Sinatra to Ringo Starr to Joey Ramone. They were aggressive, but not threatening; cute, but not conventionally handsome; sexy, but in a shy and goofy way; tortured, but too amused to brood for too long. Drunk? Yes. High? Yes. But they never were the types who steal your TV set to sell it for another fix. "They brought a group of kids—mostly girls—from their suburban towns; girls from Hercules would come to the show," Appelgren recalls. Distribution for *39/Smooth* had been adequate. Occasionally, there'd be people in the audience in the South or Midwest who'd know the band's songs well. But in Northern California, every kid seemed to own a copy.

"Sort of normal, non-punk high school girls started showing up," observed Lookout employee Patrick Hynes. "Billie Joe was like their neighborhood idol. They were ridiculed in the scene. There was this thing called the Trout Dance where a girl would stand with her arms crossed, bend her knees, and shake her head so the ponytail would shake [so she'd resemble a trout wriggling on the end of a hook]."

Sean Hughes recalls how the Trout Dancers soon became something of a liability. "They'd fold their arms and shake their heads. I think some people might have been jealous that they were getting attention paid to them by girls."

"People would kind of tease [Green Day] about it," Hynes

adds, "but I don't think anybody really believed that they weren't really punk. If there were people like that, they were in the minority."

"It was like a mini Beatlemania," Arica Paleno recalls. "The love songs Billie wrote had a big part to do with it. A lot of punk bands didn't have that same nature, and I think the girls started to pick up on that. They started to see a little Paul McCartney thing going on. They would show up and dance. It was groupie-dom, but it was cute. It was sweet. And one thing about Billie, he was never into groupies. To his benefit." Armstrong preferred the long-distance companionship of Nesser, whom he was still telephoning on a regular basis. On one hand it allowed him to focus on the band, pouring all the energy he might have expended on a girlfriend directly into Green Day. On the other hand it was difficult to take any of the Trout Dancers too seriously. Outside of Petaluma, anyway. "They were huge in Petaluma," Sean Hughes says with a laugh. "And there were all these hot chicks that were into them over there."

In spring of 1991, while Green Day was recording their first album with Tre Cool on drums, something unusual was brewing several hundred miles north in Seattle, Washington. By the time *Kerplunk!* hit stores in January 1992, Nirvana's second album, *Nevermind*—their first for major label DGC/Geffen—overtook the pop charts and seemed to make the melodic Beatles-conscious punk rock that Green Day had been defiantly pursuing for years extremely marketable. Suddenly, the commercial prospects for a young, loud, and snotty trio from the 'burbs of a major U.S. metropolis seemed limitless, whereas before, it was foolish to dream of selling 10,000 vinyl copies and touring in a bus rather than a van.

If Green Day had made a lackluster second record, they would have still stood a chance of getting further than they ever had before, on zeitgeist fumes alone. But *Kerplunk!* was yet another leap forward. The record's title may sound as if it's an homage to the Hasbro game of skill, but more than likely it refers to the sound effects resulting when you do number two from a great height. As on *39/Smooth*, the line between the scatological and the dreamy is exceedingly thin but with *Kerplunk!* it starts to feel like an actual sensibility as opposed to a symptom of arrested adolescence. Mock country corn such as Tre Cool's "Dominated Love Slave" happily coexists with genuinely romantic pop like "2,000 Light Years Away," and neither feels forced. Green Day take their "shit" as seriously as they do matters of the young heart.

Most important, the band was still enforcing good quality control. "Who Wrote Holden Caulfield?" and Armstrong's song for Paleno, "Christie Road," are both pop gems. "The twelve chunks of fun on *Kerplunk!* favor melody over speed metal aggression and lyrics of love and confusion over explosive revolutionary tracks," *College Music Journal* (*CMJ*) wrote in their January 31, 1992 issue. "The hooks in these songs are as easy to find as a broken string must be at a Green Day show. Keenly underscored by gleeful, chiming vocals and hurdle-jumping basslines, Green Day's tunes stick in your head like cat hair."

"Unlike some people, I consider Nirvana and that whole Seattle scene to be at most tangentially related to punk rock," Livermore says. "They certainly had little or nothing to do with punk as we were practicing and experiencing it in the Bay Area. Still, when *Kerplunk!* came out in January 1992, it sold ten thousand copies the first day, which was phenomenal at that time. The Operation Ivy LP, which was our perennial best-seller, had taken a whole year to sell its first two thousand." By the end of the year, *Kerplunk!* sold another twenty thousand and pumped up the sales of *39/Smooth*. College radio play added to the boost in the Green Day phenomenon.

Steve Masters, the former music director for San Francisco station KITS Live 105, recalls, "I used to do a show called the 'Local Modern Rock Block' on Thursdays, and I'd play a lot of demos and local acts' indie releases. Green Day's record really stood out [among the local bands]. And I was kinda picky."

Matt Pinfield, a college radio DJ at Rutgers in New Jersey at the time, agrees: "People just grabbed a hold of them. Eighteen- through twenty-one-year-old kids who were sneaking into bars were into Green Day. They knew *Kerplunk!* They knew *39/Smooth*. And they were spreading the word among their friends. I would run into a 7-Eleven in Jersey and someone would recognize me and go, 'Ah, hey Matt Pinfield. I'm going to see Green Day!' I think the thing that made people grab hold of it was that it had such a pop element to it. They represented a complete turn in punk from the hard-core to the pop-informed."

By the next wave of U.S. tour dates, Green Day were filling prestigious venues like the Whisky A Go Go in Los Angeles and Slim's in San Francisco. A feeling of excitement, some kind of organic buzz seemed to trail them wherever they went. After three years of struggle and lean times in crash pads, Green Day was starting to see some serious results. "They'd be playing Sluggo's in Arkansas, and it would be full of people," remembers Bill Schneider. "They'd fill it just through word of mouth."

With the royalties they were making, Armstrong and Dirnt purchased new equipment and a new touring vehicle—a converted Bookmobile. Basically, it was a van with a huge cab for storage and sleeping. They'd ripped out the shelves and tossed whatever volumes remained. The band would soon load up the battered cab and embark on another cross-country tour. This time, however, the buzz would precede them and the shows would be full. Tre's father was the sometime navigator of the Bookmobile, but most days, there was little adult supervision.

"They were like little monsters let loose on the road," Appelgren says, recalling tour life without Kiffmeyer to keep them in line. Danger seemed to find them at every stop. "I got slipped some acid from a hippie when I was in South Dakota,"

Armstrong said in 1992. "We were staying at this hippie people house and this guy comes up and he goes, 'Here,' and he put these two stupid little pills in my hand. I go 'What's this?' And he goes 'Two will do ya,' and he walked away. We crushed 'em up on the porch, and everyone in the van was waiting for our trip to come."

The psychedelic trip never came (perhaps it was a placebo). The *Kerplunk!* tour did take them to Europe for the first time, however. As they moved from country to country, Green Day saw the world like most of their friends and family members never did. It was exciting, but at the end of the night, the band felt increasingly alone and overwhelmed. They bonded, as they would when things were overwhelming, and by the tour's end, all three seemed irrevocably possessed. "It was the best thing we ever did for ourselves," Dirnt said. "We were there three months, playing on borrowed equipment every night. We played in squats. I don't think we were a tight band before we were there, but all of a sudden something clicked."

"We all saw the same new things and had the same new experiences," Cool agreed. "We shared stuff together. It was a ground-shattering, life-changing tour. Every single experience was something completely new that none of us could imagine."

It was evident to all who encountered them that Green Day was on a course for something huge. A kind of self-made cultural ripple is like blood in the water to the majors. The unprecedented press and radio play made it easy for people to catch wind of Green Day, monitor *Kerplunk!*'s sales, and place the trio at the top of their "next Nirvana" lists.

"When they came back from tour, everybody at the label was pretty much flabbergasted," Patrick Hynes says. "The roadies would say, 'It's fucking crazy. The last time we played in this town there was like fifty people and now there's three hundred.'"

"They came back home, and the world had changed," Bill Schneider says, "and they didn't really feel like they had changed at all—and they really hadn't as people or musicians—they'd always wanted to grow and go to the next level." "It was a gradual build," Appelgren says. "And we [at the label], with each milestone we achieved, thought: 'Well, gee, we can thumb our nose at the rest of the world for being such idiots before.'"

"It was only in 1993 that I started getting serious rumblings about them possibly jumping to a major," Livermore continues. "I heard rumors sometime in the early spring of 1993 and cornered Tre about it. He said they were 'talking' to a management company about the possibility of signing to a major label, and I got the whole band together and asked them what was going on. They told me they'd pretty much already decided to go for it, and not too much later, they got a deal."

Green Day had pretty much managed itself back in the Kiffmeyer days and beyond. Now they were represented by the management/legal team of Elliott Cahn and Jeff Saltzman, a Los Angeles–based firm that had been signing up modern rock acts in the wake of *Nevermind*'s success. "We all made jokes about [the band signing with a major label]," Appelgren says. "'Well if we sign, here's how we'll scam 'em.' Then it became a reality. The band said that they had authorized their team to see what kind of deal might be possible for them. I was very critical of this decision. I had this conversation with Billie Joe about how I really was concerned that if they didn't succeed, and at the time there was nothing to really make us believe that they would, that they wouldn't be able to come home again. Billie didn't finish high school. If they didn't pull this off, then that's gonna be it and they're gonna be done. I felt they would be much better served continuing to do things on their own terms and build up success and snub our collective noses at the establishment. I expressed that to Billie. He was eventually gracious, but I think he was annoyed at first. He was defensive. The way it was construed was that I had a problem with what they were doing. But Billie said, 'We feel like this is our opportunity. It's what we've been working toward. We believe in ourselves, and we're gonna do this.' I had to agree with that. I believed in them too, but I just didn't know that the world could get it."

Green Day performed their last ever show as an independent punk rock band at 924 Gilman on September 24, 1993. The show was recorded for posterity and remains a much-circulated bootleg to this day. At the time, however, the band had no idea it would be such a historical document and that they would never be formally invited back.

Chapter Six

ANARCHY 90210

In the August 24, 1993, edition of the *San Francisco Chronicle,* the announcement of a minor acquisition was made. "Warner Brothers Records won the hard-fought multi-label battle to sign Green Day, a trio of Berkeley-based twenty-year-olds that have sold an impressive 30,000 copies of each of its two albums for East Bay independent Lookout Records. The buzz on the band is that Green Day, a not so oblique reference to pot smoking, is a grassroots phenomenon poised to break big with the release of a major-label debut early next year."

At the time, Warner Brothers was widely known as an artist-friendly label, with a roster of integrity acts. Reprise, the label subsidiary for which Green Day would record, was the label founded by Frank Sinatra and was the home of Jimi Hendrix during his short recording career and of the Kinks and Neil Young during their prime. The Replacements had released four albums on Sire Records, another WB subsidiary. Sire's roster of British and American punk, post-punk, and New Wave acts—from the Ramones to Talking Heads to Echo and the Bunnymen—was legendary. R.E.M. had transitioned from cult indie IRS records to Warner Brothers three years before and were now vying with U2 for the title of biggest rock act in the world. Jane's Addiction had graduated from L.A. underground parties to arenas. The Flaming Lips had just signed and would record their breakthrough *Transmissions from the Satellite Heart* shortly thereafter. In the age of mega-selling alternative rock, Warner Brothers seemed to be the place to be. But all was not ideal inside the label's offices. Body Count, rapper Ice T's hard-rock collective, brought on serious bad publicity with their song "Cop Killer." And for every R.E.M., there were dozens of failures. Worse, the label had recently extended a multimillion-dollar vanity label enterprise with its perennially hottest act, Madonna, who was in a little slump. Everything Madonna touched was not turning into an across-the-board smash hit lately. It would be nearly two years before Maverick Records would fill up the WB coffers with Alanis Morissette's *Jagged Little Pill*. In the meantime, the label needed a boost to keep its stockholders from sweating.

In 1993, however, nobody inside the Warner offices needed a hit more than rookie A-and-R man Rob Cavallo. Cavallo came from a music business family. His father, Bob Cavallo, was Prince's manager during his *Purple Rain*–era superstardom. Like Armstrong, Cavallo grew up in a house filled with music.

"I heard the Beatles very early on, when I was two," he remembers. "By the time I was eleven or twelve, I just had to know how they made those sounds. I was just wonderstruck. I began to figure out how they played all those songs on guitar, bass, drums, piano. I had this quest to figure out how they did all that. And so I became a moderately proficient player in a number of different disciplines. Then I would try to figure out how a bunch of other bands played their songs, bands like the Stones, Led Zeppelin, The Who, Stevie Wonder, Prince, and Earth, Wind, and Fire riffs."

Cavallo moved from his native Washington, DC, to Los Angeles when he was ten. He graduated from USC with an

English degree. After he graduated, with the Clinton-era economic boom still a ways away, there were few good jobs available, even for someone with connections. Cavallo, with his stocky frame and glasses, decided he stood a better chance getting somewhere as a producer than a performer.

"I was forced with the prospect of making money," he says, "but I also played—I was in bands. But I knew I didn't really want to be a performer. I was in bands all through my teens. I was just having fun. I never actually took any of the music stuff seriously. To me it was always a hobby. It was fun to go on stage and be that kid who could play. By the time it became something that was serious—when you're twenty and you're not really faking it; you're not just a kid anymore."

"He always wanted to be a producer," says David Katznelson, his former producing partner. "When he was young, if he was given any presents or any kind of money from his father he would go right to the Guitar Center and buy equipment. I mean, granted he didn't come from a life of misery. You know, he wasn't poor, but he didn't just rely on the fact that his father was Prince's manager. He went out there, and he taught himself how to produce, and he experimented and all that kind of thing—and he read every book on it. He was a psycho student about this stuff. He geeked out."

"I ended up producing a demo for a band called Rhythm Core," Cavallo says. "Warner Brothers heard it and said, 'We don't really want to sign this, but we think this demo is good enough to get them a deal elsewhere.' And I said, 'Well, I'll just keep trying to make one that's good enough for you guys to sign.' And then they said, 'OK, you're on the staff. We'll give you five hundred bucks a week.' I said, 'I'll take it.'"

Cavallo would discover, sign, and produce bands for Warner. One of his first was also one of the best: an L.A. pop-punk act known as The Muffs. Lead by a charismatic screamer with bangs named Kim Shattuck, The Muffs (who still tour and record) are the great lost pop punk act. Their self-titled major label debut was a cult hit and very much a prototype for the platinum-selling bands that would follow nearly a decade later. At the time, however, it was another in a series of Cavallo-affiliated flops (among them an act named Sister Whiskey, whose WB debut was idiotically entitled *Liquor Poker*).

Green Day's demo came to Katznelson first, but he was unimpressed. Today, he remains at peace with his status as the man who declined to sign Green Day. "I liked Green Day, but I didn't love them. I didn't feel passionate about them, so I pretty much gave the tape to Rob," he recalls. "To be frank, I wasn't a huge fan of Billie Joe's voice."

"It was during the mixing sessions for that record that the attorney of The Muffs, who comes from Berkeley where Green Day was working, said, 'Rob, you should listen to this,'" Cavallo remembers. "I took the cassette and listened to it in my car on my way home that night—'Basket Case' was on it. 'Longview.' I loved it. Loved it right away, and I just said, 'Oh my god, you gotta let me see these guys!'"

While their manager and lawyer were fielding offers, the band was back off the road, living and rehearsing in a basement apartment in a turn-of-the-century Victorian house on Ashby Street in Oakland. From the outside, the place looked elegant. Inside, it was another squat.

"I never personally witnessed any of the A-and-R guys giving their pitches there," Livermore said. "Though I did hear stories about limos pulling up in front of it."

The ceilings in the Ashby house were so low that people who were more than six feet tall could seriously hurt themselves if they weren't careful. "It was a classic kind of guys' place," recalls video director Mark Kohr (who would later shoot the band's "Longview" video in the living room). "Mattresses on the floor, milk crates, plywood furniture, and a tiny practice room with corkboard soundproofing."

"There were just a lot of bizarre drinking antics going on in that house," Jeff Ott recalls. "Fishing for people off the roof with fishing poles, and literally we'd put a wallet at the end of the line."

When Rob Cavallo pulled up to Ashby Street in the summer of 1993, he was just a few more failed projects away from taking that bait. "I was failing—I got my job in 1987, I signed Green Day in 1993," Cavallo says today. "I hadn't done anything of great merit in six years, except for maybe helping Black Sabbath on a song in *Wayne's World.* But you know what was great about Warner Brothers at that time and still is today? They really allow you the chance—they saw something in me that I didn't even know was there.

"If you ever see the 'Longview' video, that little room, except for the fact that they painted the walls blue and red, was pretty much exactly what I saw as an A-and-R guy. I sat on a bucket looking up at Mike and Billie, who were in the exact same positions as in the video. There was no monkey. I saw them play for about forty minutes from my seat on the bucket, from that upward camera angle. And I thought, oh my god, I love these guys. I remember they heard that I could play all those Beatles songs and they said, 'OK, let's jam,' or something. They got me stoned, and I started playing guitar and we jammed. We had a good time. There was an immediate chemistry."

Armstrong was a fan of Cavallo's work on The Muffs record and was impressed that he did this at a major label. The fact that Cavallo, unlike most A-and-R executives, could actually play, surely helped his pitch as well.

"I think I might have been the first person he told that they got signed up as Green Day with the first major label," says Tre Cool's old school friend Zann Cannon Goff. "I used to work at Whole Foods Market. And I was cashier. Tre would come in regularly because he was living near there. So he comes in one day buying a bunch of cookies and chips and stuff and looking all glassy eyed, and he's like, 'You'll never guess what just happened.' And I'm like, 'What?' He's like, 'This guy from Reprise records just came over and he got us stoned and signed a record deal with us. We're gonna be really big.' And in the back of my mind I'm like, 'Yeah right, what-ever.' Who the heck out of Willits is gonna be on MTV? Yeah right. Then it was three months later and there he is on MTV. That day was the last time I saw him. I was pretty damn shocked. Definitely jealous. Since there was someone younger, bigger, and richer, and more famous than I am. And that's al-ways a bummer."

"Things got a little more complicated once we became suc-cessful," Armstrong told me in 2005, during our *Spin* sit-down. He was recalling with some understatement those first few months when word started to get around that the band were leaving Lookout. It was one thing to go to the pizza place and be recognized by a total stranger. It was another matter entirely when those total strangers called you some very unkind names.

"Punk rock is elitist," Fat Mike of NOFX explains, "and people in punk rock feel like 'this is our scene; we don't want other people liking this kind of music.' When I was a kid and X signed to a major [Slash/Warner Brothers], I was pissed too. We felt privileged and lucky to see X at the Whiskey or Green Day at Gilman Street. And when they go to a major, you're never fucking seeing them at Gilman Street again. You're go-ing to go see them in Oakland Coliseum. And I've seen Green Day at Oakland Coliseum, and it's no fucking fun."

"It was a huge backlash," Appelgren remembers. "It was huge around here at least. There were Mohawk kids out there protesting in front of their shows out in Petaluma."

It was unspoken but abided that Green Day were no longer welcome within Gilman (whose pre-entry list of rules read and *still* reads: "We do not support racism, homophobia, or major label bands") to perform or even to watch their friends perform.

"Lookout couldn't get them into the Fillmore in San Francisco. They didn't have that torque. Green Day needed a bigger label, bigger management, bigger distribution," says Arica Paleno. "They almost had no choice [but to leave.] It was supply and demand. And I remember them saying, 'Well, everyone is going to hate us. They're going to shun us. I don't know what's going to happen.' And it *was* really bad. Gilman had that no-rock-stars policy. And Green Day wasn't allowed around anymore. They went from everybody's darlings to everybody's joke. 'They sold out. They're totally against what we represent as punks.' Whatever. Fucking bullshit."

"Billie Joe told me he felt the backlash bad enough that if he went to Gilman he disguised himself with a beard," Jello Biafra says. "To me I thought that was very, very sad and not a good statement on how the punk underground devours itself. These guys are human beings. When somebody becomes well-known, other people sometimes reduce them to this subhuman thing. You know, they're not a friend anymore; they're an 'it.'" *MRR* ran anti–Green Day letters and snarky comments they'd received from readers apparently with glee. (When contacted for this book, the person at the other end of the line almost reflexively snarled, "Not interested," before hanging up abruptly.)

"Can you imagine what it feels like to pick up that magazine [*MRR*], something you totally respect, and read all these fucking opinions about you?" Armstrong asked *Spin* in 1994. "That's what the Gilman Street scene is," Brett Gurewitz says. "Its very identity is tied up in being other than the mainstream. It can't embrace them anymore. Or it isn't anything."

Much of the loudest protest was headed up by an extremely irate punk named Brian Zero. Banners and petitions designed to officially excommunicate the band were circulated, but many were so over the top they were easy to dismiss. The editorials in *MRR* and general day-to-day trash-talking was a bit more down to earth and, therefore, much more hurtful.

"It was mostly just a lot of talk and snarky comments in fanzines," Livermore says, downplaying it somewhat today. "But the band may have taken it a lot more seriously and personally because they were young and that whole Gilman scene meant so much to them." Livermore was one of Green Day's loyalists, defending them in his own *MRR* column by casting the blame not on Green Day directly, but on those moved to bileful indignance by their actions.

Never ones to take a blow without delivering one, the scrappy punks fired back at *MRR* in one of their first national cover stories. Speaking with *Spin* in 1994, Armstrong snarls, "Tim Yohannan can go and suck his own dick for all I care. He doesn't know what the fuck he's talking about. I've never waved a punk-rock flag in my life."

But it was clear that the barbs had left wounds. Feelings were hurt at a time that should have been completely celebratory.

"There were a lot of Northern California punk rockers, and probably from some other places too, who weren't happy," Rob Cavallo acknowledges. "I remember there was a banner that was made that said 'Fuck Green Day' or 'Green Day go home' or whatever. It was definitely a big deal for Green Day to take that step because there were many, many fans and friends of theirs who thought they were selling out. But I also know that the majority of those fans, when they heard *Dookie* (later on) realized, wow, they didn't sell out. They just made a really good record, you know?"

"What I warn bands about to this day is that the trouble with major labels is that when you sign on the dotted line, you cease to become an artist and from that point onward you are their employee," Biafra says. "You are employed to generate pop culture for them to make money off of, and hey, they might even pay you. And in the meantime you get to be a star. Once you figure out there's all kinds of sacrifices in high-visibility stardom and pressure on your ass, and that maybe you don't like it anymore, it's too late. You're on the treadmill, and they want more product and want to exploit you any way they can."

Still, he dismisses those who put the fatwa on Green Day with equal disdain. "The entire underground scene was livid at Green Day, and deep down their crime was being successful. And my attitude was look, OK, in my case I didn't want to go this route, that's fine, but we all knew from the get-go that some day the public was going to discover and embrace this music. It was too good not to have reached mass success eventually. It was an inevitability. And I tell people to this day, look, the reason Green Day and Rancid and Offspring and Bad Religion and NOFX and the others got where they are is because like it or not, they're good at what they do."

This topic enrages Courtney Love for personal reasons. Her late husband, Kurt Cobain, had massive ambitions but also an odd guilt about selling out or violating the unspoken but brutally enforced punk fundamentalist dogma.

"Fuck the nineties for that shit," she fumes today. "Fuck the nineties for that shit 'cause lookit now! I remember getting a Lexus for 60K and getting eggs thrown at it! We couldn't even have a motherfucking Lexus when we had 10 million in the bank? I hate my generation for that. Rules? Yeah, yeah, yeah, yeah. Rules schmules. Fuck that. I mean fuck it. And now the whole context of celebrity has changed and we get no credit, those of us who semi-abided by those rules or were forced to abide by those rules. God, I don't want to sound bitter. I don't really care anymore but having to live through the nineties and live through those crass rules . . . anti-successful, anti-brand, anti-consumer, there's no level of credit. Your credibility should come from your lifestyle, your wholesomeness, your values, from how you conduct yourself, your level of decorum, all of which Billie Joe has abided by very well. His level of decorum has always been really good. Polite to his elders. Polite to his peers. Tim Yohannan never accepted me either."

Yohannan, it should probably be pointed out again (in the band's defense), was from a middle-class background. Historically, it's been much easier for people with a certain degree of privilege to carry on in a dogmatic fashion. Armstrong, Cool, and especially Dirnt knew what it was like to eat macaroni and cheese for dinner every night and sometimes not have money for gas. To refuse a major label deal on principle is easy if you've never seen your parents working in restaurants. "I did not realize until I talked to the Green Day guys at length that they came from far less advantaged backgrounds than most of the people in the punk underground and most of the more-radical-than-thou," Biafra says. "When I talked to Mike Dirnt about it, he finally kind of snapped at me a little bit and said, 'Look I've got money, and I bought my mom a house so she doesn't have to live in a trailer anymore.' I've also noticed this from the beginning in hip-hop culture versus punk culture: Even among the more political rappers, they're more accepting of money and fancier cars and showing off a little wealth and whatnot. And granted that turns my stomach, but it's also a reflection of people who grow up not having a damn thing, and entertainment culture dictating down to them, just like Motown did before, that it's much better to dream of being super filthy rich than to systematically, brick by brick, get yourself out of poverty."

"It's so white to worry about things like that," Armstrong said in 2005. He had more than a decade to reflect on it and was then liberated from Green Day's paralyzing dual personality syndrome. He ultimately decided that success, even in the values-driven world of punk rock, was really nothing to be ashamed of. Earning it didn't mean you were superficial or treasonous. "Hip-hop guys are so much more dangerous and so much more willing to take risks in music in a lot of ways because they're not afraid to be successful. It's embraced. That's what you're supposed to be. You're supposed to be a superstar. In rock 'n' roll, and especially alternative rock music, it's sort of looked at as if you're not supposed to be up there. It's taboo. And it ends up making for conservative music because all of a sudden you feel like you have to have all these rules and are not really a rock star."

"It all depends on what you call punk," Brett Gurewitz said, after I posed the "Cred" question to him. "Let's take the word punk out of and call it hip. Take an artist who's this obscure, unknown artist and he's just very hip. Say a graphic artist like Jean-Michel Basquiat. And then he explodes and then he dies. Now everyone knows him. Is he still hip? I wouldn't say so. He's collectible. To me the thing about Green Day is they just write really great songs. And they just keep doing that. I think they're just a great rock band. Do I think they're punk? Yeah, I mean I do. But I guess the question nowadays is what does it mean to be punk? For me it's kind of like asking me if I'm Jewish. Like, I hate Judaism, I hate the Old Testament, and I don't believe any of that. But I'm still Jewish. Punk is almost like an ethnicity, you know what I mean?"

"Tim Yohannan sort of spun a spider web for himself and then tightened it further and further with each passing year," Jello Biafra laments. "He admitted to me at one point when *MRR* was all hard-core all the time in terms of what they were the champions of. He told me, 'You know, sometimes I get kinda tired of what we're playing on the show and when I'm home I just want to listen to Billy Childish.' Even till the very end you could flip through the *MRR* record collection and find a Slim Harpo album or something in there that Tim never felt he could get rid of. I think he kind of confused it a bit in the end."

Even as they trashed Green Day, everyone, punks and non-punks included, waited to see what the band would come up with given this opportunity. Before most of the world even knew Green Day's name, in certain circles, their third album was already wildly anticipated and the band, not yet old enough to drink legally, was feeling the pressure.

Green Day behaved characteristically, doing what they always did when things around them became painful. They closed ranks together and focused on new songs. They had reason to be excited by the material that they were coming up with for the controversial, major label debut. "They all really focused," David Katznelson remembers. "I think they had something to prove."

"We kind of evolved," Armstrong said in 2005. "I loved *Kerplunk!*, but I think at the same time we didn't have time to think it out or define who we were with it. There was something that happened to us when we signed to a major label [Reprise]. I became really focused on the songwriting. I really want to make something that defines who we are and that has a statement behind it, even if its like an anti-statement. All the major label bands that came from punk rock had sort of failed on major labels, so it became a real gamble."

"My mantra as a producer at that time was, I want you to sound like the best version of yourselves. I think *Dookie* is a really good snapshot of what Green Day sounded like at that time. And that's why I think it works: because it's honest. That's not only why it works, but also why we didn't get killed. I didn't turn out to be the evil record producer who sold out Green Day's sound."

You can tell, literally, from the very first noise that you hear—a sharp Tre Cool drum beat preceding the opening track, "Burnout"—that the Green Day/Cavallo partnership would take them very, very far. Listen to *Kerplunk!*, then cue up *Dookie*, and the difference in production is remarkable, like an old Triumph bike that's had its engine cleaned.

Its title may be self-deprecatingly scatological but the music is nothing if not confident, almost struttingly so. The first verse, if you read into it at all, can only seem ironic now: "I declare, I don't care no more . . ."

Dookie, conversely, marks the emergence of a band who are finally committed and positioned to destroy all comers. It gets even better quickly.

Track two, "Having a Blast," is all about an explosive-strapped suicide bomber's giddy nihilism (in the early nineties this kind of thing could still seem darkly funny). "Chump" is another piece of effortless snotty speed-pop. On any of the earlier albums, it may have been a centerpiece. A single. Not here.

As it fades out, the walking bass line to "Longview" rolls in. It's lounge jazz–derived, but you can also tell that it too is wired to detonate. The drums roll easily and Billie Joe's adenoidal tone thickens and slows down a bit towards a conversational tone. "The lyrical content of it was supposed to be almost like a Pink Floyd moment," Cavallo remembers. "Where you have a guy wondering how fucked up he really is. There was a version of it where we put this doctor speaking in the background. He's talking about all these various sexual dysfunctional diseases related to impotence and things. That's something that is brilliant and is on tape somewhere but didn't make it to the record."

•

"There's this lyric that goes 'Call me pathetic, call me what you will,'" Patrick Hynes recalls. "When they'd play the song at their shows, before *Dookie* came out, their friend Eggplant from the audience would shout, 'What you will!'" And so when they recorded it, if you listen really carefully you can hear him shouting it. They brought him into the studio just to do that. If you listen on headphones, you can hear it."

"It's one of those songs where you can really feel the scene," Cavallo observed. "You can just know what Billie's talking about. 'I've lost my motivation. Where is my motivation?' You know, 'I'm smoking my inspiration.' When it all fades down at the end, sort of like as he describes after you've masturbated or whatever, you're kind of relaxed and then that soft guitar riff comes. It just sort of fades away."

It's perfectly realized punk rock. Alienated but longing to be understood. Adolescent but weary. "Longview" is Green Day's first immortal single, as potent to teenage ears today as it was a decade ago and as it will be a decade from now. And it's not even the best song on the record. "Welcome to Paradise" sounds crisper and even more furious than it did on *Kerplunk!*, now that the scary crash pad in West Oakland is even further behind him.

The girl in "Pulling Teeth," a love gone wrong lament, is Dirnt's girlfriend Anastacia. Dirnt, ever accident prone, cracked his elbows after a pillow fight with her. "I was running and turned around and hit a beam," he recalled at the time. "It was lucky though; I happened to be ducking down. If I hadn't I would have crushed my face." The basic metaphorical equation of actual pain of a nearly crushed face with heartache works better than it should.

"Basket Case" is the album's high point and probably its most enduring track. Like "Longview," it's a worrying bit of teenaged self-inventory; a plea for help with a little bit of pride that our narrator, paranoid, stoned, or both, is not like anybody else. Structurally, it's simple three-chord pop punk, but there's an authority to how it's played that seems less fully formed on previous exercises. Green Day's segue from influenced to influence really begins here.

"She" is another Beatlesque pop song that has as little to do with *MRR*-approved punk as possible. Its lyrics are gentle and poetic. A portrait of a disenfranchised punk girl: a recurring theme in Armstrong's lyrics that extends all the way up to "She's a Rebel" and "Extraordinary Girl" on *American Idiot*. "Are you locked up in a world that's been planned out for you?" he asks his screaming (albeit "in silence") subject. Green Day's female audience exists largely because of songs like this.

"Sassafras Roots" is a throwback to *Kerplunk!*'s Gilman-approved stylings. The harmonies on the "wasting your time" refrain aside, it is the record's only real regression, especially when sequenced into "When I Come Around," destined to be *Dookie*'s third (and biggest) single. Even less typical, "When I Come Around" is a near-ballad with a slow, boozy groove. "No time to search the world around, cause you know where I'll be found . . ."

When people accuse Armstrong of being a wannabe pop idol, they usually wave their fingers in this direction. Like most of *Dookie*'s tracks, this could have been a hit for anyone. It's yet another piece of classic songwriting, but there's something inescapably juvenile about it. The kind of lyrics that seem written to be scrawled in homeroom notebooks. This, of course, is still all wonderful. "Coming Clean" picks up the tempo but doesn't allow us to graduate.

"Seventeen and strung out on confusion . . ." Armstrong sings in his best Paul Westerberg-esque tone. It's the band's most overt homage to the Replacements.

"Emenius Sleepus" hints at the distance the band have put behind them, touring, signing with a major label, becoming ever more famous. Like "Longview," it's an exploration of alienation but this time from someone who has a way out of the bedroom. It's a nice bookend. A different kind of tension.

"In the End" has a country-punk shuffle to it, hinting at Armstrong's upbringing in Rodeo. "F.O.D." ("Fuck Off and Die") closes the record with a snort, a kiss off, until Cool emerges, after a two-minute pause with a lisping bit of psycho-stalker novelty, called "All by Myself," another *Tre song*. "He has many of them," Cavallo says. "Enough to make a comedy album? Definitely."

The levity was not something the new partners reached with ease. "There was some angst in the studio," Cavallo recalls. "They had never been produced before. The longest they had ever spent in a studio was three days in a row to make *Kerplunk!*" (Green Day, it should be noted, receive co-producer credit with Cavallo on *Dookie* as well as the subsequent albums on which they've collaborated). To reduce the tension, they'd hit the bar at the Mexican eaterie down the road from the studio. "Tre wasn't old enough to drink, but they would serve him."

The mixing of *Dookie* was completed in late 1993 in Los Angeles. Armstrong, Dirnt, and Cool returned to the Ashby House to rehearse for an upcoming tour with Los Angeles punk heroes Bad Religion and to spend some catch-up time with their girlfriends both home and elsewhere. Armstrong spent many of his free hours on the telephone with Adrienne Nesser. Although they weren't yet a couple, Armstrong filled much of these conversations encouraging her to come to California to visit him, temporarily, at first, then perhaps permanently. Nesser was still in school and couldn't get away easily. He already had commitments on the road. They agreed that she would visit immediately after the tour and just before the record's release. Neither of them could have possibly guessed what was about to happen next.

•

"When I turned in the record, the people at the company immediately said, 'Oh, we've got something here guys,'" Cavallo remembers.

The band returned to Los Angeles a few weeks later to discuss various marketing details with then Warner Brothers Reecords marketing director Geoffrey Weiss. Weiss had heard and loved the new music but was expecting a trio of sneering, Johnny Rotten–worshippers. He encountered three extremely young and semi-overwhelmed individuals. "It was slightly intimidating to be in the Warner Brothers building for anybody," Weiss says, "because it was this giant construction full of all these gold records and all these legends of the music business. Anybody who comes from a punk rock background was looking at us saying, 'Jesus Christ, look at all this money, look at all this corporate rock culture.' Onstage, Billie Joe just had this sort of 'look at me' quality to him that was so unlike what he exuded in person, where he was almost modest."

With the songs completed, it came time for Warner Brothers and the band to decide just how to sell this clearly strong product to the world. Warner Brothers, seizing on the trio's cute appeal, obviously wanted a band shot for the cover. Green Day had other ideas.

"We had a great art department. We had every great photographer, every great illustrator, we had books for everybody," Weiss says. "But that wasn't the point. The point was that this band came from a very specific culture and we had to honor that."

The cover of *Dookie* is probably the goofiest cover ever to grace a ten-million seller. Fanzine artist and local musician Richie Bucher's apocalyptic rendering of a fecal bomb exploding over the Bay Area features everything from Patti Smiths's hair armpit from the *Easter* album sleeve, to a shoutout to Black Panther Huey P. Newton and Black Sabbath (quoting from the song of the same name) to dogs and monkeys throwing their own poop.

"I think that they saw a fanzine cover for Eggplant's 'zine *Absolute Zippo* and they liked it," Bucher says today. "Billie Joe just told me that it was gonna be called *Dookie* so I had that to work with, the whole shit theme. That was all I really needed. I had just had this little germ of an idea, and I did a drawing—you know, with the plane coming down and swooping over and dropping shit. Then I saw characters around and just drew them in. The dogs were like something I associated with shit, being a kid, when there was dog shit all around and you throw it at one another and stuff. And monkeys at the zoo, you know, it's just all stuff I remember from being a kid. Shit-oriented stuff."

Once pre-release detailing had begun, Green Day went back to the Bookmobile to head with Bad Religion. "I remember hopping on the Bookmobile and hanging out with them each night after the shows," Gurewitz says, "Jerry Finn was remixing the *Dookie* record and mailing them CDs. This was the days before broadband at Starbucks. And we'd sit in the Bookmobile and listen to the mixes, and the guys were really into Jerry's mixes. I remember when all of that was going down. I remember thinking the songs were huge hits when they were playing them every night live before I'd even heard them mixed."

Bad Religion have a hugely loyal fan base, especially in California. Green Day had been filling small clubs on their most recent outings, but there were two- and three-thousand-seat venues filled with hard-core punks. Supporting Bad Religion could be a challenge to a lesser band, but Green Day were on fire, every night. One by one, they converted the suspicious, ripping through one soon-to-be-released *Dookie* raver after another.

•

"The show at the Warfield was where Green Day finally delineated themselves for me," agrees Gina Arnold. "Before that, they were merely part of that Gilman amalgam." "We went out to the Hollywood Palladium and saw them open for Bad Relgion," Jesse Malin (then of New York punks D Generation and now a solo artist) says, "and suddenly the place just erupts, and they're putting on such an amazing show. I was really super-impressed. I didn't even stay for Bad Religion. I would later talk to Billie and he'd say, 'Yeah, it was our first really big gig,' but you couldn't tell. It's a big, tough, spread-out room to play, especially opening for Bad Religion, an L.A. band."

"L.A. is a city that Bad Religion kind of owns," Weiss says. "For a band that didn't have a high profile, at least as far as I knew, it was shocking how well they went over. The audience went bananas for them. [After seeing this] my goal was to have a successful record, which to me meant that if we sold a couple hundred thousand records, it would be fantastic. I remember when Rob was making the record, I asked Tre what his goal was. And he said, 'Oh, I just want to sell half a million copies,' which I thought at the time was a ridiculously ambitious thing to say."

The band shot the video for the "Longview" single in their basement apartment on Ashby Street. Video director Mark Kohr was a young protégé of filmmaker Tim Burton (*Beetlejuice, Edward Scissorhands*) and hired for the shoot. "I think the reason why they called me is because I lived up there and I did a whole bunch of videos for Primus, which they had liked," Kohr says. "So I think that Green Day said, 'Well, get the Primus guy.'"

Kohr was familiar with the Ashby house, as it was on his way to his chiropractor's office. During the first meeting with the band and their management, Kohr sat quietly and listened as the band brainstormed. "We'll just do what we do in the apartment. Watch TV. Rehearse." Budgetary constraints necessitated a performance video, but Kohr encouraged the band to get creative with their suggestions.

"[After that] Billie would say stuff like, 'Hey, you know, I was wondering if you could get a monkey to be sitting with me on the sofa,'" Kohr says. "And I said, 'Sure.' And then there was stuff like, 'Mark, I was wondering if we could shoot like a guy, this friend of ours, as if he were masturbating.' And I said, 'Sure.'" Kohr added mirrors to the walls and painted them bright blue and red. Designed to introduce Billie Joe, Mike, and Tre to the world, the video wisely relies on close-ups and emotions reflected in the song. "I listened to the lyrics and broke it down as I wrote scenarios," Kohr says.

The band's clothes are their own, but Kohr did insist on a hair and makeup person. "I, of course, wanted them to look as real as possible," he says, "but a big white pimple? I don't know. Sometimes stuff like that needs to be dealt with, so it's always good to have someone there." A stunt couch was also necessary for the climax, in which Billie Joe leaps up and begins stabbing through the cushions. "They didn't want to stab their own couch," Kohr laughs.

The shoot lasted only two days, but by the end of it, the young director had perfectly captured the band as appealingly approachable—cute but intense young punk personalities. The day after the shoot, events beyond any director's control or vision transpired that would, albeit indirectly, thrust Green Day even closer to modern rock's center stage.

On the day that Billie Joe, Mike, Tre, and their pet monkey were romping for the cameras on Ashby Street, Nirvana leader Kurt Cobain was dead on the floor of his Seattle home. "We all went home and the first thing that was out on the news the next morning was that Kurt Cobain had killed himself," Kohr remembers. "I went into the living room where we shot, and Billie said, 'Oh my god, did you hear that Kurt Cobain killed himself?' and I said, 'I know, it's wild.' And he said, 'Such a bummer.' He was really affected by it."

Although both bands toured their respective indie releases across the United States around the same time, Cobain and Armstrong never met. Cobain knew of Green Day only vaguely. He caught an early '90s Pinhead Gunpowder show in Seattle. Although an avid, indie punk singles collector, he was most likely distracted by that pesky voice of a generation thing, when Green Day were touring *Kerplunk!* His widow, Courtney Love, insists that Kurt would have been impressed, however. "The title is about poo poo," Love says. "It's toys for boys. I'm sure Kurt would have dug it."

Armstrong, for one, was a big Nirvana fan. Like Cobain, he came from a little and often-maligned town, far from a major city but close enough to long for it—Cobain was raised in Aberdeen, a logging town outside of Seattle. Armstrong's family life was once blissful, then, suddenly, destroyed by a parent's death—Cobain's destroyed by divorce. As a songwriter, Armstrong related well to Cobain's secret love of power pop, and he knew what it was like to be vilified for it once it started getting too much attention. "I remember standing right next to him at a Nirvana concert about two years ago," Armstrong told *Entertainment Weekly* in December 1994, just seven months after Cobain's body was found. "I really admired him. I just sort of sat next to him and looked at him, and I was like, 'Oh fuck it.' I just walked away. I'm sure he had people hounding him all the time so I chose not to do it."

Interestingly, Armstrong had been taken to the Nirvana concert in 1993 by an A-and-R representative eager to sign Green Day to Cobain's label (the major DGC).

"To some extent, he's like Jesus to me," Dirnt told *Spin* that same year. "He died for my sins, so I could sign to a major label." As it happened when Operation Ivy disbanded five years earlier, a void was left in the culture (this time, worldwide, as opposed to just regional) for someone to fill. Green Day were again ready to step in. "All of a sudden there was no one there," Armstrong says in our 2005 *Spin* interview. "It was like there was no leader anymore."

When *Dookie* was released on February 1, 1994, the initial shipping sold out, unexpectedly pushing the release right to the top of the Billboard heat-seeking chart. Warner Brothers had severely underestimated the demand for the new record, and the rush to ship more created the kind of waitlist buzz that still can't really be planned.

Although it overperformed out of the gate, *Dookie* took some time to become a phenomenon. The album's X-factor, the thing that separates platinum-selling hits from diamond (10 million copies) shifting cultural touchstones, could be its odd kid appeal. (Ironically, the image of an Ernie doll, held up by a fan on the album's back jacket live shot, had to be air-brushed out of reprinted copies of the record because it risked infringing on the equally beloved Sesame Street character's copyright).

"Rock 'n' roll had been hijacked by this sort of critical, college and upward mindset and Green Day spoke to nine-year-olds," Weiss says. "Probably because the videos were so colorful. I think 'Longview' just had a beat that really made sense to little kids. They'll kill me for saying this, but the same way as the Spice Girls did. Or if you were nine in 1964, the Beatles were on TV, and they were in your face and they had that youthful exuberance. Green Day had that. Nirvana didn't. Nirvana was angsty. If you were nine, that angst did not make any sense. On the *Dookie* tour it seemed like there were lots and lots of nine-year-olds in the audience."

"I think X-factor is always the same, which is people," then Reprise label president Howie Klein says. "Those songs on that album are undeniable. What people tend to not understand is that Billie Joe Armstrong is one of the great songwriters of our time. I believe that in the future he will be looked at as a really important songwriter the same way Joni Mitchell is and the way Bob Dylan is . . . and Neil Young is."

There's a reality and a conviction to Armstrong's vocal delivery that immediately resonates as honest, and it seems that no matter where they grow up, at a certain point in their lives, this is what pre-teens and teenagers are craving from their increasingly confusing world. "It goes back to his upbringing," Klein says. "Billie is real. Everything about him is real. Which, of course, permeates the music and permeates his persona and his public everything. He experiences it in his life and that informs his music. To me he's like a modern-day Woody Guthrie. That's how I've always seen Billie Joe Armstrong. And I've never told him that 'cause I thought he would just think I'm out of my mind."

Early modern rock radio support didn't hurt things, as far as bringing on those who'd already been through puberty. Los

Angeles–based station K-ROQ, to this day the alpha dog of the entire country as far as taste-making and hit-picking goes, played the hell out of *Dookie*. The rest of the nation followed. "I remember first hearing 'Longview' on K-ROQ. I was driving down Topanga Canyon Boulevard, ten thirty at night, and I heard the song and I had to pull over," Cavallo says. "I thought to myself, 'Holy shit. This really could be a hit.' It was one of the first times it was played. Of course, I was calling the radio station [requesting it]. I called about ten times, 'Hey, this is Steve from Canoga Park . . .' "

•

The Offspring are a band from Southern California and don't really sound anything like Green Day. As with Nirvana and Pearl Jam a few years earlier, one group is a fluke but two groups with massive hit singles in the same time period, from the same (gigantic) state, and with origins in classic punk constitutes a movement. While the Offspring played Gilman in their pre-fame years, the two bands, it's been widely reported, are not fans of each other (the Offspring politely declined to be interviewed for this book). It may be personal. It may just be social chemistry. But at least some of their perceived animosity must have to do with being bound together and chucked into the zeitgeist as "the platinum punks." *Smash*, the Offspring's breakthrough (ironically on cred-to-spare indie Epitaph) sold a nearly identical amount of copies as *Dookie* (although in recent years their cultural importance and commercial stock has fallen noticeably).

"With grunge," K-ROQ program director Kevin Weatherly notes, "there already started to be at that time like the fourth, fifth, sixth generation of grunge. So Green Day came along, and it was this like really fresh, authentic, you know, punk sound but big hooks. It was young but it was real. It felt that what Nirvana was to grunge, Green Day was to the new punk movement. Obviously, there were some punk bands in the eighties but they never really broke out of that. Being kind of defined as just a punk band. *These* were punk bands that really wrote big, fat hit songs."

"*Dookie* was one of those records where we had to refrain from putting five songs on the radio," K-ROQ's music director Lisa Worden adds. "When we got the album it was like, 'Oh my God! Oh my God!' K-ROQ's famous for putting on too many things and the label freaks and it just pulls us back. But we did put 'Basket Case' on right away too."

As "Basket Case" made a steady crossover from modern rock to pop radio, the band headed back to Europe, this time as headliners. "They couldn't believe what was happening," says Bryan Jones of the band Horace Pinker, a frequent tour opener during the *Dookie* promotional push. "It was surreal but they were just trying to have a good time, just trying to ride the wave and make the most out of it. It was weird because there were still some places where *Dookie* hadn't hit. Like Belgium. Nobody knew who they were in Belgium. There were maybe two hundred people there. I remember after the show, we were sitting there watching them play and we're just like, 'Wow, this is the last time we will ever see them in front of, you know, two hundred people.' After the show, I saw Billie out on the sidewalk, smoking, and nobody was bothering him. I was thinking you know, 'This is probably the last time this guy can sit here on the sidewalk and just hang out and nobody will fuck with him.' "

"What happens to a band that gets that popular," David Katznelson wonders. "I think Green Day handled it pretty well. I can tell you what happens to the *label*. The label is back in a place where they need to be, where they have a number one band. There's nothing like breaking a number one band. You can bring back bands, and have bands maintain themselves, but you have a band that no one's ever heard about coming out of nowhere that looks sexier than you could ever look. And the label loved it. And Rob was the golden boy."

"It was in the spring of 1994," Cavallo says, "and they'd just been back from touring in Europe. I picked them up at the airport, and I got them all in a rental car and said to them, 'Guys, I gotta tell you something, you know, all the indicators point to the fact that you're gonna sell a couple a million records even though we've only sold a couple hundred thousand or two hundred and fifty thousand. Just the trajectory of the single, all the research a record company can do is telling us that it's gonna be pretty fucking huge.' And Tre, who I love, says to me, 'Well of course it is, Rob. What did you expect?' And I said, 'Yeah, but I think it's bigger than you even think. And it's bigger than we ever thought.' There was silence for the first five or ten seconds. They were letting it sink in. And then we just started hopping and hollering and having a great time. But it's always an adjustment. There's always a 'Holy shit, what did we do this time?' Every time you take another step in your career, especially if you're stepping into the limelight to be famous and to do something, it changes—if you're smart, you realize what's happening is it's actually changing you and it's changing what you mean to your fans and it's changing what you mean to yourself and it changes what you mean creatively. And I think they were always really smart and aware of that and they realized what it does is it sets up a new challenge. And I think that was a good signpost that our conversation was met with sort of pensive bravado."

"Everything after [*Dookie*'s release] was completely unpredictable," Armstrong told me in 2005. "I remember everything being scary. It was a really sensitive period for us. We were affected by the fame . . . kind of in a negative way. We should have just looked at our record and said, 'We made a great record. And we know that, and we don't have to justify anything. Stick to the music.' But we were all twenty-one, twenty-two years old. We just started trying to get into the bar scene. All of a sudden, you walk in and you're this famous band. You're in this shithole bar, and you're like, 'Wait a minute I just want to have some drinks.' And so-and-so is trying to talk to me and so-and-so wants to pick a fight with me."

The band had one another through it all and would filter out any weird energy as they did in the past: by employing an insular sense of humor, tended to during countless nights alone in a van in the middle of nowhere.

924 Gilman Street and the ethics they took with them even after they were banned had always made Green Day feel somewhat invulnerable to schmoozers and celebrity-hungry hangers on. But now they felt completely outnumbered. There was no real protection from these people once they crossed over into super-fame.

It was around this time that Armstrong realized that he wanted to be with Adrienne Nesser for good. Perhaps this new and relentless exposure to suck-ups and industry jivers had a positive effect in that it refined the twenty-two-year-old's sense of what was really real and what was fleeting. After four years of unconsummated courtship, Armstrong finally succeeded in pairing up with his teeange crush.

"I still had my set of friends," he says. "I loved them. I loved Adrienne. She's the best thing that's ever happened to me in the whole world and that was all I needed."

"I think Billie was honestly head over heels for her. It was almost like they were stepping up [with everything else], so I think growing up a bit with regard to relationships was a part of it," David Armstrong says. "Everything was happening at once. Traveling, and then a brand-new wife that was pregnant." Armstrong's sister has a similar theory. "I think he felt untethered," Anna says. "And Adrienne was somebody he could put in his pocket in a lot of ways. He could carry his family or someone close to him with him at all times. He loved her and he knew that she loved him. I think when he was feeling alone she made him feel that he wasn't."

The band were booked all through the summer, with promotional appearances set up at every major city stop. When

Armstrong proposed to Nesser in June, he knew he didn't have a lot of time for wedding planning or a honeymoon. The couple married in a small (and by all accounts, extremely short) ceremony at the Claremont Hotel, Berkeley's poshest, just a few days later, on the second of July, 1994. The bride's and groom's families and the members of Green Day and their girlfriends made up the wedding party. The following day, Nesser found out she was pregnant. The day after that, Green Day joined the fourth annual Lollapalooza tour. "They just sort of signed up for everything all at once, you know," recalls Jason White. "Billie got married within maybe a few months, I don't know, after the record came out. And then, you know, right after he got married they find out she was pregnant. Same thing happened to Tre with his first wife, Lisa. And Mike got married to his girlfriend Anastacia right after that as well. Maybe they needed to feel grounded because they didn't know what the hell was happening to them."

"I remember at one point after we'd had giant hits with 'Longview,' 'Basket Case,' and 'When I Come Around,' the company really wanted to come with 'Welcome to Paradise' as the fourth single. And it was getting tons of airplay," Geoffrey Weiss recalls. "But the band wouldn't let us put out a single of it, and they wouldn't let us work it and they wouldn't let us make a video. And we kept trying, and Billie Joe's whole rationale—I kept saying, look, we can sell more records. He didn't care. To him the song was about a period of his life—I think he was ambivalent about rerecording it. I just kept saying, 'Look, people wanna play this song, people wanna hear this song, we'll sell more records.' And he was like, 'It's a lie. I can't do it.' So, I never really saw him as being unambitious; I just saw him as being like, 'I do this for a very particular reason, and I'm not gonna change my thinking about it no matter what.'" "Welcome to Paradise" became the radio smash that never made it to retail, further proof that even the band could do nothing to slow down their success in 1994.

Ironically, for all the rancor it inspired, *Dookie*'s impact on the world had a positive effect on the Gilman Street scene as well. True to form, Green Day opted to tour the United States with gay punk rockers and Lookout signees Pansy Division instead of a fellow Warner Brothers act who might have benefitted from their support. As the venue sizes increased, so did the jock to punk fan ratio, and the band seemed to delight in making them sit through numbers like "James Bondage" and "Denny (Naked)." "There was this club," remembers Pansy Division's John Ginoli. "It was a bowling alley, held six hundred people, and it was way sold out. There was somebody in line who was wearing a belt that said 'White Power' and they were like, 'Oh, no.' Just the kind of people they do not want at their show. So they got some security people, the whole band went out there with their security, everybody's in line, they confront this guy, and say, 'We don't like your belt.' And the guy's like, 'Well it doesn't mean anything.' And they're like, 'Well, it better not. We're watching you.' And they had the security guys there looking up the guy. So I thought that was nice to try to defuse the situation in advance. And to have the message be out there that [racism or sexism] was something they wouldn't tolerate."

Lookout Records' fortunes soared thanks to increased sales of the EPs and the first two full-lengths, as well as a general interest in Bay Area punk rock. "Our sales went from several hundred thousand dollars a year to several million almost overnight," Livermore says. "It was a bit of a shock, but I think that's one area where being older was helpful: Because I'd been around a while, the large amounts of money coming in didn't seem quite so big a deal as it might have been if I were still in my twenties. That being said, I found myself dealing with enormous pressure to spend more of that money on marketing and promotion from bands who thought that was all that stood between them and being the next Green Day."

"Green Day and the Offspring have both had long careers," Fat Mike says today. "But there's fifty other punk bands that totally blew it: Jawbreaker or Jawbox, punk bands that signed to a major in 1995 and disappeared because their regular fan base disowned them, and they never got popular."

Soon, Green Day were selling out arenas all over the United States, but they applied some of their Gilman-nurtured punk humanism to this surprise superstardom, accomplishing what fellow early nineties superstars Pearl Jam could not do (with much less fanfare too): offering their young fans cheap concert tickets. The math was pretty simple. By starting with a low ticket price (thanks to low overhead) they were able to allow an agent to tack on a fee and still keep tickets in the fifteen- to twenty-dollar range.

The band applied an equal measure of fiscal responsibility to their new fortunes as well. For much of 1994 and '95, they were simply too busy to slow down and spend their new wealth unwisely. They also carried around a measure of Gilman-guilt, which would, for a few years anyway, prevent them from fully indulging in the rock-star privileges and toys now available to them. Indulgences, however, were very few. They wore the same clothes. Drank the same beer. None of the members of Green Day came from money, and financial security for themselves and their families (old and new) was a primary concern.

While it was somewhat easy to keep their business sound and practical (having come from essentially nothing), controlling the spin was much more difficult. As *Dookie* sold and sold the attention thrown on the band would only get more intrusive and weird.

Green Day played *The Late Show with David Letterman, Saturday Night Live, Late Night with Conan O'Brien*, and MTV, increasing their profile and teen friendly lovable Marx Brothers of punk identity. Once mainstream print media, sensing a trend "punk redux," came around, and a thousand "Young,

Loud, and Snotty" or "It's Not Easy Being Green Day" head-lines were born. The days when they were only being bashed in 'zines seemed swell by comparison.

Dookie was too big to be just a great record. It was now both critically adored and insta-contextualized. Like *Never-mind*, it was read into as a generational statement. "This is music for people with raging hormones and short attention spans," *Time* magazine wrote in June 1994, "for the sort of kid who, as his burrito rotates in the microwave, impatiently frets, 'three minutes is an eternity.'" "Beavis and Butt-Head have started a band and it's called Green Day," crowed *Rolling Stone* in their "Hot Issue" of that year (Green Day being named Hot Band). *Entertainment Weekly* would later note (in December of that year) the phenomenon of the trout dances writ extremely large. "Call it Anarchy 90210. The punk rock of yore may have been the property of gloomy subterraneans, Orange County surfers, and jackbooted British thugs, but these days the Clearasil club is learning to mosh."

Dookie-mania brought equal measures of absurdity and mayhem to the band as they criss-crossed the United States in the summer of 1994. Lollapalooza was dizzying if only be-cause they were slotted into an opening slot in the harsh day-light. At the previous Lollapaloozas this main stage slot was usually occupied by a band just grateful to perform for a few hundred kids, and get their merch booth out on the lawn. Green Day, who agreed to the spot before *Dookie* exploded (they replaced Japanese noisecore heroes The Boredoms, who played the first leg), were now the biggest draw on a bill headlined by Beastie Boys and Smashing Pumpkins (and once earmarked for Nirvana). Thousands of kids clogged the venue at 1 p.m., and immediately made a break for the toilets and concession stands following Green Day's all-too-short set.

"Once again, the organizers of this whacky affair decided to put the cart out before the horse," the *Music Connection*

LOOK FOR LOVE

"Billie Joe"

Recorded by "Billie Joe" on Fiat Records

Lyrics by James J. Fiatarone
Music by Marie-Louise Fiatarone

$1.25

Sheet music for Armstrong's "debut" single, "Look for Love"
Courtesy of John Roecker

Billie with some of his earliest admirers, 1982
Photo courtesy of Marie-Louise Fiatarone

Tre Cool, aged 13, and muscle-bound (with Lookouts bassist Kain), 1985
Photo courtesy of Larry Livermore

"Can I Offer You a Soft Drink?" Teenage Mike Dirnt (with his pal Eddie on the wall), 1987
Photo by Sean Hughes

Dead Kennedys at Mabuhay Gardens in San Francisco, 1981
Photo by Chester Simpson

Higher Education: Operation Ivy perform a set on the UC Berkeley campus, circa 1988
Photo by Murray Bowles

Sober revelers inside 924 Gilman Street
Photo by Murray Bowles

Green Day performing at the Gilman, circa 1990
Photo by Murray Bowles

Flyer for Green Day and Rancid show at the Gilman, 1993
Artist Unknown

Billie Joe, Tre, and friend at the Gilman, circa 1990
Photo by Murray Bowles

Acoustic, topless, otherwise seriously rockin' circa 1990
Photo courtesy of Arica Pelino

Billie Joe's beloved Fernandez Stratocaster, better known as "Blue"
Photo by Ken Schles

Billy and future wife Adrienne
Nesser outside the band's apartment,
1993
Photo courtesy of Rob Cavallo

Young, soon-to-be-major-label
artists, possibly not stoned, 1993
Photo by John Popplewell / Retna Ltd.

Getting ready to record *Dookie*, 1993
Photo courtesy of Rob Cavallo

In the studio with *Dookie* sound engineer and co-producer Doug McKean and Rob Cavallo, (seated at board l-r), 1993
Photo courtesy of Rob Cavallo

Inside the bookmobile, 1993
Photo by Ken Schles

All in the family: Bookmobile driver and father of Tre Cool poses with the band, 1993
Photo by Ken Schles

Not yet headliners: On tour with Bad
Religion, 1993
Photo by Ken Schles

Never happier than when rocking: Billie Joe
works the crowd, 1994
Photo by Kelly A. Swift/Retna Ltd.

Backstage at MTV Video
Music Awards, 1994.
Photo by Kevin Mazur/WireImage

Giving their all onstage at Madison Square Garden, December 1994
Photo by Chris Cassidy/Retna Ltd.

Mudstock: Onstage during their infamous Woodstock performance, August 1994
Photo by Neal Preston/Retna Ltd.

A riot of his own: Billie Joe
storms the Boston Hatch
Shell's flowerbed, September
1994
Photo by Arthur Pollack

Billie meets his hero, Joey
Ramone, at the MTV
Video Music Awards
*Photo by Kevin
Mazur/WireImage*

On the set of "Redundant" video, 1997
Photo by Mark Kohr

Tagging Tower Records during their notorious in-store, New York City 1997
Photo courtesy of Warner Bros Records

Tonight you're in Green Day, bud. Pulling fans up for "Knowledge" on the Pop Disaster Tour, circa 2002
Photo by Bob Gruen / Star File

Are we not Green Day?
The Network, 2003
Photo by Jay Blakesberg/Retna Ltd.

Writing lyrics, 2003
Photo courtesy of John Roecker from the film Heart Like a Hand Grenade

Billie Joe lays down vocals
for *American Idiot,* 2003
Photo courtesy of Rob Cavallo

On the set of the "American Idiot" video, summer 2004
Photo courtesy of Warner Bros Records

With John Kerry on the set of *The Late Show with David Letterman*, September 2004
Photo by John Paul Filo/Landov

The band rehearse
backstage before a show
on the *American Idiot*
tour, 2005
Photo by Dean Chalkley/
NME/ IPC+ Syndication

American Idiot world tour: Live in Japan
and UK, 2005
Top photo by Yuji Ohsugi/WireImage, Bottom photo
by James Looker/ NME/ IPC+ Syndication

Backstage at Irving
Plaza, September
2004
Photo by Marc Spitz

Destined for greatness: Billie at age 5 and Billie today
*Top photo courtesy of Marie-Louise Fiatarone, Bottom photo by Joshua
Prezant/Retna*

observed at the time, "and scheduled Green Day, the hottest act on the roster, to *open* the event."

A Kohr-directed video for "Basket Case" (shot in a still functional lunatic asylum) found even more favor at MTV than "Longview." Still, by the time they left the stage for what is, to date, still their defining performance, they would be the most popular rock group in the world. Green Day were huge, and not just in Petaluma.

The Woodstock 2004 Arts and Music Festival was designed to celebrate the twenty-fifth anniversary of the original, legendary gathering of hippies and freaks in Upstate New York in the summer of 1969. Billed as "three more days of peace, love, and music," the event had the air of a marketing ploy, but the bookings, a combination of classic rock godheads such as Dylan; Crosby, Stills and Nash; Peter Gabriel; and Santana, with modern rock and metal favorites like Nine Inch Nails, Metallica, and the Red Hot Chili Peppers—with a good measure of crunchy, jam-friendly beardos, old and new, from Blind Melon and Blues Traveler to Country Joe McDonald—were smart and the 300,000 fans who traveled to Saugerties, New York, in early August were eager to drop $130-plus on some more history . . . and a tie-dyed T-shirt or leather cuff.

Sheer audience demand was the only thing that made Green Day a likely addition to an otherwise punk-free bill. "I went there with really low expectations and came out overwhelmed," Armstrong told the *Los Angeles Times*. "It was the closest thing to chaos, and complete anarchy, that I have ever seen in my whole life."

The event that helped turn Green Day into a household name almost didn't happen. "There were people who wanted them to do it and people who didn't want them to do it," Geoffrey Weiss says. "I think I fell into the camp of people who didn't want them to do it because I thought that

Woodstock was something from a long time ago; it was for hippies, it was part of a previous culture's iconography. Why on earth would this band that stood for this important musical subculture finally breaking through want to rely on the imagery of another time when they were so clearly of this time."

As they did twenty-five years previous, the skies over Upstate New York opened on Day Three and each tribe—hippie, Goth, punk, hip-hop head—was drenched with rain. By the time Green Day hit the stage at about three in the afternoon, the 830 or so acres of farmland became a mudfield, and the audience was completely covered. "Welcome to Paradise" was the set opener. As he sang, some mud and spew-covered souls found this ironic choice a bit offensive and began chucking the sod at the band.

"Come on you assholes, throw some more," Armstrong egged. He grabbed a piece of mud and stuck it in his mouth as he sang. The crowd lost it at that point and the gunk-fire tripled, then quadrupled, turning the expanse between the giant stage and the dank pit brown. This was Green Day's biggest show yet. With the pay-per-view audience, they'd be playing to millions. Their families and friends were watching at home in the East Bay. Their peers were watching from backstage, and here they were . . . covered in dookie.

As they did whenever life tried to shit on them, they turned it into a triumph. "It worked out well because of the mud fight, and it got incredible international coverage," Weiss continues. In the middle of it all, Mike Dirnt was beaten senseless by a panicking and overzealous security guard who, what with the sky being brown and solid, mistook him for a stage-rushing fan. It was hailed as a refreshing bit of anarchy in an otherwise calculated bit of mall-ified counter-culture; proof that Green Day and their fans really were interchangeable. "Who gives a shit about that," Dirnt said at the time. "The fact of the matter is that it was a great show. That was an unfortunate incident." Besides, Dirnt had done far worse to himself in the past. By the time the headliners, the Red Hot Chili Peppers, took the stage that night nobody was talking about the headliners, the Red Hot Chili Peppers.

"Woodstock was nuts," says Anna Armstrong, who'd been, along with the rest of Billie Joe's family, more or less agape all year over Green Day's ascent. It began with the shock and thrill of hearing "Longview" on local modern-rock station Live 105. "We'd sit around listening or calling in. That was huge. But with Woodstock, we were thinking, 'Look at this crowd. And look at Billie, how he's able to interact with them and control them like that.' I always knew Billie was a showman, and I knew [watching him] that he wasn't afraid to be up there."

Woodstock's impact on the band's fortune's were seismic. In one perfect synthesis of planned stagecraft and a few priceless accidents, Green Day broke out of the modern-rock box, just as they had broken out of the indie punk box the previous year. They were now pop stars, household names. "I always call it pre- and post-Woodstock," says the band's former publicist Jim Baltudis. "Literally the following Monday the phone never stopped ringing. It was just a complete one-eighty from a publicity standpoint. We had eight lines, with the blinking buttons all blinking at the same time. We'd come back from lunch and there'd be fifteen new messages about people wanting to talk to the band. It was such a turning point. The sod throwing and Mike's tooth getting knocked out just created a huge buzz that was organic and huge at the same time. I remember watching the performance and thinking, 'Oh my God. This changes everything.' Press [for *Dookie*] started out as a well-crafted plan with the best intentions. Then it became crisis management. We just went from crisis to crisis."

"Everything we did, if we did something smart, made them

sell more records," Weiss says. "If we did something dumb, it made them sell more records. It sort of seemed like an unstoppable juggernaut. If you put them in front of the cameras or in front of the culture in that year, everything worked."

"I decided I couldn't handle Green Day as big as they were, so I left the country," Arica Paleno says. "I went to Europe, but there were huge posters of them everywhere. They were on the sides of double-decker buses! I said, 'My God, I wanna escape this band.' So I go to Central America and I'm in Nicaragua on a mountain and I hear a guy on the local radio station saying *'Verde Dia! Verde Dia!'* and then something from *Dookie* comes on. I was thinking 'Goddammit. It's three a.m. I'm on a mountain. There aren't even mirrors here. I have to look in silverware to put on lipstick. And here's Green Day on the fucking radio. I went all over the world trying to bail on this band, because it was too emotional.'"

Dookie surged up the Billboard charts post-Woodstock, eventually peaking at Number 2. When the tour hit Boston, just three weeks later, for a free September 9 radio promotional concert at the Hatch Shell of the Boston Opera House, Green Day notched up their second riot inside of a month.

"I was never worried about the amount of people," says Kurt St. Thomas, then program director for WFNS, the local rock station that organized the event. "But after seeing Woodstock [on television] I said 'OK, kids are gonna mosh and they're gonna get really rowdy.' And we had done shows on the Hatch Shell before but never with a band like Green Day. It would always be like a reggae band or something like really mellow."

When more than 100,000 impatient punks began crowding the Hatch Shell area and began chanting "Green Day" while opening act The Meices played, local authorities started to panic. This wasn't exactly Altamont East but there was a nervous-making tension already in the air, an hour before headliners Green Day were set to perform. "So now they're like, 'We're gonna fucking pull the plug,'" St. Thomas remembers. "That's it. I just remember it kept getting more and more intense." The crowd responded to these threats with chants of "Pigs suck! Pigs suck!" and "Hell no, we won't go!"

After several announcements to calm the crowd (a few made by Armstrong himself) Green Day began their set but it soon became clear that the situation was beyond containment. By the seventh song in the set, which was "Longview," Armstrong himself was caught up in the energy of the moment. "Billie Joe jumps off of the stage, [goes] down into the flower bed and starts pulling flowers out of the bed, and basically that's when all hell just erupted. And that was it. They just shut the power down. Green Day ran off the stage down into the bottom of the Hatch Shell, and then bottles just started flying."

The *Dookie* North American tour finally wound down in New York City, shortly before Christmas. When 1994 began, Kurt Cobain was alive and Green Day were a club act with a hot buzz on them. The band members were all single and living off their tour money and indie royalties. By December, they were a Grammy-nominated, arena-rocking trio of young millionaires with wives and fiancées. The press considered them spokespeople for the Beavis and Butt-Head generation. In March of 1995 Billie Joe and Adrienne welcomed their first child, Joseph Marciano Armstrong, into this new world. The couple would have a second son, Jakob (middle name "Danger") in September of 1998. Tre Cool had married his girlfriend Lisa Lyon and in January he too became a father, of little Ramona. They were twenty-two years old, but much of the rest of their lives seemed already set for them.

"I'm just exhausted," Armstrong told *Entertainment Weekly* that December. "Totally. We've outdone ourselves in a serious way. I have insomnia problems anyway, so it's hard for me to sleep. That's the main thing I'm looking forward to. I'll probably sleep for the rest of the year."

Whether or not he knew the rest of the year was only two weeks long at the time is questionable. It had been a truly dizzying run.

Chapter Seven

INSOMNIACS

Insomniac, the follow-up to *Dookie,* was one of the most anticipated rock releases of 1995 (it vied for that status with the
Smashing Pumpkins' double disc *Mellon Collie and the Infinite
Sadness*). As Green Day convened to begin recording their new
material, once again with Rob Cavallo, they were still shell-
shocked by the events of the previous year and struggling
with questions of identity and purpose. In the past, life was
only about making music and staving off boredom. There was
more to it now: family, money, image, pressure.

Armstrong, Dirnt, and Cool all purchased houses in suburban Oakland. They could have lived anywhere in the world,
but the Bay Area provided them with a sorely required feeling
of solidity and familiarity. "I'm sure one day I will leave," Armstrong reasoned. "But I've been an East Bay kid my whole life."

"Billie wasn't sure how to enjoy his success, or if he even
should. 'Should I enjoy this or should I be miserable,' " his sister Anna remembers. "And yeah, they really did close ranks. I
think that's one of the reasons why they stayed up in Oakland
instead of moving to L.A. It was a really traumatic time. It
even changed his relationship with us. You'd be excited about
your brother's success and want to talk about it, but he

wouldn't want to talk about it. It'd be taboo. Like there was something wrong with selling ten million records."

Sean Hughes simply remembers them disappearing. "They never flaunted their status," he explains. "They were just around [Rodeo] a lot less."

Attempts to live the normal lives they'd never really known were made but even in the suburbs, people knew of Green Day. Grocery shopping was difficult if there were any teenagers around. During the day, when they were all in school, Armstrong, a walker, would travel to the store to get the newspaper and a cup of coffee in the early afternoon, and find himself grilled by the middle-aged proprietor. "When is the new record coming out?" "I don't know. Probably this fall. Thanks for the coffee," he'd reply, before beating it. The world, only a year ago, seemed wide open as they moved through it like an army. Now, it was shrinking. Billie Joe wrote some of his new material while staying up all night with his young son. These sleepless nights inspired the album's title.

As usual, only Green Day could relate to what they were going through. The band, now a mini-corporation, put several of their friends like Bill Schneider on the payroll as techs or assistants; but even their closest friends had a hard time providing any empathy over the fact that they were now husbands and fathers, much less international rock superstars.

Family and rock, or rather family vs. rock, was the make-up of their daily lives. A new song was due, but the refrigerator was broken and "Didn't it need to be fixed? Can we get someone to do that? Am I supposed to do that? How do you fix a refrigerator? How do you write a hit when you're *trying* to write a hit? *And* fix the fridge?"

Paranoid notions swirled around Billie Joe's, Mike's, and Tre's heads as they tried to focus on one thing at a time. The group were always business minded out of necessity. John Kiffmeyer had taught them that. Now Green Day *were* a business.

"One question we get asked a lot now," Mike Dirnt

complained in a 1995 *Spin* interview, "is 'How much money do you make?' When I was younger, I actually asked that question to my mom's friend. My mom took me and slapped me in the face and said, 'Do not ask that question. It's none of your business.' Sure we make money. We make plenty of money. And it's peace of mind for me to know that I've bought my mom a house and that my little sisters don't have to live in a trailer anymore."

"I have a vague recollection of intentionally trying not to talk about money with them," Jeff Ott says. "At some point after *Dookie*, they said, 'Who should we give money to? The accountants say we have to give away money for taxes.' And I kind of remember feeling like, 'Oh, that's why I avoided all that just to keep that stuff clear.' So I don't know how they dealt with it, but I didn't really wanna deal with people about money at any point in my life. Really, I still don't."

"They certainly made a lot of money and they certainly were able to buy houses and cars and things. Although that really wasn't where their mindset was necessarily at," Cavallo says of the post-*Dookie* period. "They actually were saying to themselves, 'We've made it now. What are we gonna do?' And their main response to that was to prove to everybody that they still rocked."

Their fourth full-length and second Warner/Reprise effort, *Insomniac,* recorded over the summer and released on October 10, 1995, is commonly referred to as Green Day's "reactionary record." Galled that they'd been tagged as teenybopper punks after cross-country van tours and an indie career that lasted nearly twice as long as Operation Ivy's, the band indeed felt that they had to prove themselves "still punk."

Whenever possible, they opted for the raw and the in-your-face over the tweenie-friendly. The cover, a collage commissioned from Winston Smith, for example, was entitled "God Told Me to Skin You Alive."

"I got a call one day and it was Tre and he asked, 'Hey, we

were wondering if you still might be interested in doing a record cover for us,'" Smith recalls. "And, I said, 'Oh, sure, come on over. You can look at some of the pictures I got.' And he and Bill and Rob Cavallo, who was their producer, really nice guy himself, came over and hung out for a couple hours and went through big piles of stuff. We went out for a pizza and looked at different stuff and at one point I asked, 'So how's it going? You guys got a day job or did you sell any records for your last record?' You know, 'cause I had never seen their names all the time in *MRR*; all I could see was other bands in the Bay Area playing here and there. And he says very calmly, 'Well, you know, our last record sold about nine million copies.' I nearly fell down. I thought they had printed them up and were peddling them out of the back of the VW microbus."

The video for the first single, "Geek Stink Breath," was a perfect piece of career-suicidal behavior. With bloody dental surgery footage, straight out of a punk rock *Marathon Man*, and the band appearing only on static-marred television screens, it was hardly the makings of a blockbuster.

"It's open to interpretations from all sides," director Kevin Kerslake says of the off-putting image, and whether or not the metaphor of career-ing as pulling teeth applies directly or implicitly. Still, with its ". . . and I'm picking scabs off my face" chorus, it's clear the band knew this wasn't one for the nine-year-olds to sing in the bath.

"It was a harder record, *Insomniac*," says Brent Burghoff, who engineered it. "A darker, harder record. And I think that was maybe the answer to some of the massive success and whatever comes along with it. [As they recorded] I saw a lot of release going on, so to speak."

"Consciously or unconsciously, the band probably didn't want to be the hit-making machine," Weiss says. "That was my perception of why they would choose a song like 'Geek Stink Breath' to come back with [after *Dookie*]. I actually thought it was a mistake."

"Geek Stink Breath" is actually a great single. It's a chugging, mean-spirited rocker about the ravages (dental and otherwise) of crystal meth abuse. The drug was, at the time, the Bay Area's signature illegal narcotic, brewed in bathtubs by bikers and tweakers and prized for its cheap and intense high. Speed is great if you're a trucker or studying for the SATs. Exalting it is not so good if you're the punk pinup from the cover of *Tiger Beat*. Armstrong knew this well too.

"They chose it, I think, to take some of the heat off them," Weiss says. "My perception was that the band had been a little bit freaked out by how big they got and they wanted to reassert how punk rock they were and that's why they made that record."

"OK, here's a band that is coming off an album that sold probably [nine] million records; I mean it was insane," says K-ROQ's Kevin Weatherly. "And so there were huge expectations when that album came out. And 'Geek Stink' was the first track and a lot of times the first track coming off of a hugely successful record gets the benefit of the doubt. And the momentum of just the benefit of that doubt can drive it up the charts. You know, that song, for us, was a good solid track, not a huge slam dunk."

Shortly before the record's release, the band cut ties with management and lawyer, Jeff Saltzman and Elliot Cahn, and decided to boil down their retinue even further. They were one of the biggest bands in the world, with a world tour on the way, when they decided to take on the task of self-managing their careers. Saltzman and Cahn may have been distracted by the formation of their own label, 510 Records. With Green Day already more than established, they focused most of their attentions on younger bands like the ska act Dancehall Crashers. This didn't aid in closing a rift between Green Day and their representation that had been growing for some time.

"I think the problem with Jeff was that he didn't listen to

them," says Mark Kohr. "510 is the area code of Oakland, or Berkeley, and at the time it just felt kind of tacky. At that time the band were concerned that they would lose their cred. So there was friction. They were stressed out."

"I think their mechanism was to shut off from the world for a while," says Jim Baltudis. "Every other phone call didn't have to be from Elliot or Jeff about some issue that maybe, perhaps they weren't at the stage of maturity to deal with. A lot of responsibility came with that new success. I've seen it happen with artists like Prince. You know, Prince doesn't want to deal with the issues that he has at Warner Brothers, so he changes his name to an unpronounceable symbol. This is what happens when you're surrounded by a bunch of yes-men. Attorneys or whatever. The mentality level shifts. I think it was probably really scary for those guys, and they managed it the best way they could. They eliminated certain things that they thought were responsible for it all."

In an interview with the *San Francisco Chronicle* in November 1995, Armstrong is asked whether it's still difficult to write about being defiant and disaffected given his level of success. "I'm not exactly defiant, but there's still things that anger me," he replied, citing racism, and police brutality.

Armstrong knew, however, that unlike before, his gripes were guaranteed an audience. Any score he wished to settle, he could drag out now before literal millions. And so we get *Insomniac*'s most talked about (and least played) track, "86." Armstrong smartly inhabits the mind of one of his own Gilman Street critics as he fires back at the punk fundamentalists who've banned him for life.

What brings you around?
Did you lose something the last time you were here?
You'll never find it now
It's buried deep with your identity

So stand aside and let the next one pass
Don't let the door kick you in the butt

There's no return from 86
            —lyrics reprinted by permission

The focused wit ranks it high on the list of great "fuck you to the old scene" songs (Bob Dylan's "Positively Fourth Street" still resting at the top of that one).

In an article that heralded the release of the *Insomniac* album while at the same time questioning Green Day's edginess now that they were big money-makers, *The New York Times* observed that the world "was their mosh pit." It wouldn't be for long.

Although the Dancehall Crashers never really capitalized on it, ska had replaced pop-punk (mach 1) as the new old genre. Although *Insomniac* debuted at number 2 (a ranking it took *Dookie* months to reach) and would be certified platinum by January, it was, like Nirvana's *In Utero*, almost willing itself out of the charts. Warner Brothers were expecting huge returns. Although burned by the lukewarm public reaction to the new record, they threw their support behind the band for better or worse.

Remember, there were always two sides to Green Day, and one of them—the ambitious inner rock star—was certainly shaken that they'd succeeded so effortlessly at . . . well, failing. It's easy, especially when the world is watching, to say, "Oh, I don't care about show business." The fact that they all had families to support, bills and taxes to pay, and the expectations of their fans and record label to meet wasn't nearly as important as the fact that, at least in part, they secretly *did* care. They simply wanted to control how small they got. Or how big. And the part of Green Day that wanted, or needed, to be big was secretly stung by *Insomniac*'s commercial performance.

"You know, when it came out and didn't sell as much as *Dookie,* I think it spun their heads around, like all of a sudden they're failures," Anna Armstrong Humann says. "[After that] Billie'd be hateful towards other bands. He'd be real negative. I don't know if it was ego or insecurity." The Smashing Pumpkins (who met both commercial and critical expectations with their *Mellon Collie and the Infinite Sadness* record) were a frequent target of Billie Joe's snide, private put-downs. Green Day's inner punk could dismiss the Pumpkins as glorified arena rockers, full of pomp but hollow inside. Green Day's latent Queen fan could only burn with jealousy. It'd be another full decade before the trio would "out" the latter side of themselves.

"We didn't just sign them because they had a couple of cute tunes," Howie Klein says today when asked about the label's loyalty. "They weren't Hanson. We were going after artists who we believed in, who have a vision that we can buy into and who we can help. Coming off this gigantic record *Dookie,* would we have liked to sell more records? Sure. But their work was not suffering. They were still doing really good work so who cares? Not for one second did I lose a nano-millimeters' worth of faith in Green Day."

Happily, Canadian former child star Alanis Morrissette's *Jagged Little Pill* album was about to become the next Warner-affiliated ten-plus million-selling modern-rock phenomenon. If this took any heat off of Green Day remains unknown. Radio play for the album's second single, "Brain Stew," enabled Green Day to move another million units in early 1996. *This* probably calmed some suits.

Recorded live and sequenced (also live) into the two-minute thrash-fest "Jaded," its melody appeared while Armstrong was humming to Joseph late one sleepless night. "We put 'Brain Stew' on and you know," Weatherly says, "it took a minute, but then it ended up probably being one of the biggest Green Day songs for K-ROQ that they've ever done."

Song by song, *Insomniac* is pretty thrilling. It's easily worthy of *Dookie,* with pummeling punk tracks like "Tightwad Hill" and "Walking Contradiction" ranking with some of the best songs they've come up with to date.

Green Day launched a world tour in support of the release early in 1996. The shows were booked into sports arenas, but the spark didn't seem to ignite this time around. Perhaps it was too soon after the extensive *Dookie* tour. Although always ambitious, Green Day still didn't seem 100 percent comfortable with their size and popularity. It would be something that would take them another decade to finally come to terms with. "We were becoming the things we hated," Armstrong said. "Playing those big arenas. It was beginning to not be fun anymore."

As they had done before, Green Day took care to keep ticket prices low and many of the shows were sellouts. However, several cities saw the band's drawing power thin out a little. The sellout shows were fine, but the smaller attended concerts seemed to be filled with fair-weather fans.

"When kids used to come to our shows, they used to come like a community, to hang out and be part of a punk atmosphere," Armstrong complained to *BAM* that year. "Now it's more like 'Alright, motherfucker . . . entertain my fucking ass right now.'"

Perhaps even more difficult than the ennui and the decreasing box office was the pain of leaving their wives and young children behind. For three young men with varying degrees of unstable childhoods, this must have been especially unsettling.

"Billie used to make these speeches on stage about how much he missed his son. Nobody could understand what he was saying," Dr. Frank Portman says (His band The Mr. T Experience provided support on this tour). "The whole thing of touring at that time, anywhere, but particularly in Europe, was finding a phone that worked; it was the most difficult thing. I remember a couple of nights in the middle of nowhere in Germany or wherever, and Bill, Tre, and I trying to find a phone so we could call our wives at home."

"I'd still rather be the station wagon kind of parent," Armstrong says today. "You know, like going to Wally World. I just wanted to be a normal dad."

This was not an easy feat, despite the fame and ability to absorb the long-distance bills. The European leg of the *Insomniac* tour, in late 1996, was canceled before its completion, and without much ceremony. The band, claiming exhaustion (surely mental as much as physical at this point) flew home to be with their families and tried one more time to balance family life with their careers.

Chapter Eight

"SHIT HAPPENS"

Another year passed quickly and by 1997, the members of Green Day were well into a long period of actually enjoying their hard-won luxury. It was impossible, however, to credibly supply another barrage of ferocious punk rock from the suburbs. The new album needed to somehow reflect their current state, although if it did so honestly, what would people think?

"Having a son has changed my ideas about life," Armstrong said at the time. "I am a father and I am a husband and I have this relationship but at the same time I want to be like an arrogant rock 'n' roll star. The two roles definitely clash."

For the third time, Rob Cavallo was brought in to sort through the three dozen new songs Armstrong and the band had finished since the aborted European tour. Despite *Insomniac*'s relatively disappointing performance, a new producer was never considered for what would be their next Warner Brothers release, *Nimrod*.

"Well Rob had been with those guys since the beginning so he's like their mentor," says Chris Lord-Alge, the acclaimed studio veteran (who would later come in to mix both *Nimrod* and *American Idiot*). "He's the George Martin of Green Day. He keeps those guys on the leash."

"They've always asked me to do it," Cavallo shrugs. "I

think they're the kind of guys who are very loyal, and I think they're very good guys. I think that they look at things like—it is definitely hard to get into their circle. But if you do get in, you're in."

There was one caveat, which the band and Cavallo did discuss at length. *Nimrod* had to be different. Essentially, Green Day, who could write stellar three-chord/two and a half minute punk rock while on the bog, were becoming bored with being Green Day. Although *39/Smooth* and *Kerplunk!* had both been certified gold by 1997, most of their fans had no idea just how long they'd been making records.

"[*Nimrod*] is the record I've wanted to make since the band started," Armstrong said at the time. "I was always wondering when I was going to get to make my 'London Calling,' and I decided the time was now." Whether or not it achieves "London Calling" status (it doesn't), *Nimrod*, with its horns, strings, and sheer size (it's nearly twice as long as *Dookie*) is surely not fenced in by provincial punk rock constraints. *Nimrod*, if nothing else, stands as a genuine transitional record, a gateway to astonishing things down the road, and in many ways a farewell to the youth that had marked them as a band so deeply from Sweet Children onward.

The new songs took four full months just to record (unspeakable in genuine punk-dom), and after a point, the process drove the band—holed up in the city's Conway Studios and sleeping inside the Sunset Marquis (a notorious rock-star playground in West Hollywood)—to drink and worse. As sessions stretched from noon to two in the morning every day, the spirited foosball tournaments around the studio's table were hardly enough to calm the demons. "One night one of us was walking down the halls knocking on people's doors while naked," Dirnt said. "Another one of us tried to pick a fight with someone from another band," Armstrong remembered. "Let's just say someone from an Australian band who's not very famous anymore." (Pretty sure it wasn't Men at Work.)

Tre Cool chucked his hotel room television set out the window and cackled as it shattered on the pavement below. "There was a lot of glass," Armstrong observed. "You have to live that arrogant lifestyle every now and again."

Cool was even briefly linked to actress and serial rock-boy poacher Winona Ryder, perhaps the strongest evidence of Green Day's submission to the rock life.

Unfortunately, the band's inner punk (whose turn it was to take the back seat this time around) was not there to keep a lid on the cliché overload, and soon the dookie began flying.

Although the band officially deny this, it was strongly rumored that on Oscar Night 1997, while acclaimed French actress Juliette Binoche was onstage collecting a Best Supporting Actress award for her extremely earnest work in the highbrow war drama *The English Patient,* as she thanked the Academy, she had no clue that Mike Dirnt's buttocks were extended, baboon-style, over her balcony—she had the misfortune of having been given the room below a very restless bass player. Dirnt's turd plunked onto Binoche's terrace and waited for her to return home. "She was so pissed she tried to get us thrown out of the hotel," Dirnt said. "As they say, 'Shit happens.'"

Fortunately, for all involved, the band were no longer managing themselves under such conditions. Pat Magnarella was hired to manage them, with Cavallo's father, Bob, overseeing the affairs in an unofficial capacity. Magnarella was, at the time, also managing Weezer and the Goo Goo Dolls. "It was just too much to deal with," Armstrong said at the time. "I wanna write songs. We didn't go around and whore ourselves to any other management. [Magnarella and Cavallo] were conveniently there. We happened to luck out. There was no contract signed. It was pretty much a handshake and a nod and we had a manager. Pat's the main guy, and Bob is sort of like the management guru."

"If we were Muppets," Dirnt clarified, "they would both be Jim Henson."

All eighteen songs that made the final sequence of *Nimrod*

are good (Green Day have never released anything truly rank), but only a few seemed worth the effort and expense. "King for a Day," a cheeky, Pete Townshend–esqe lyric about cross-dressing enlivened by ska horns and a bass line cribbed from Otis Day and the Knights' version of the Isley Brothers' "Shout!" (the band acknowledged this during their *American Idiot* tour, often segueing into the fraternity row classic). With third-wave ska act No Doubt now trumping them as the biggest modern rock band going, the track seems a wicked wink in that direction, as if to say, "We can do this too. It's not hard." "Hitchin' a Ride" opens with Middle Eastern strings courtesy of Petra Haden (then of That Dog) and proceeds to brutally (and hilariously) recount the on-again, off-again wagon jumping that the band themselves were dealing with as they veered from fatherhood to rocker-hood and back. "Nice Guys Finish Last" could be a throwback to *Dookie.* It's a neat melody, with a spirited bass line by Dirnt. "Take Back" is one minute and nine seconds of hard-core jollies. "Platypus (I Hate You)," actually a rather dark song, may just have the best rock title ever (Thank heaven for parentheses).

Nimrod's rightful centerpiece is "Good Riddance (Time of Your Life)," an unexpected piece of mature reflection that would return the band to the Top 10 on the Billboard Hot 100 singles. With a tentative false start and a strummed, campfire riff, it's not a power ballad . . . just a ballad. Like McCartney's "Yesterday," although credited to the group it's basically an Armstrong solo performance, vocals, acoustic guitar, and the strings Cavallo added. Wimpy by hard-core standards, sure. But it is also a crucial middle finger to convention, something fresh and risky and honest, something crucially by *Nimrod*'s standards punk rock. "Good Riddance" has its roots in the Gilman days. Armstrong began it shortly after getting dumped by Amanda. He wasn't confident enough at the time, however, to insist that Green Day record or perform it. He'd shelve it for three years and leave it unrecorded for nearly seven. "Supposedly Billie had brought an early version of it into the studio when they were recording their first album and John had told them 'No,'" Chris Appelgren says. Kiffmeyer, using the old *MRR* criteria, ruled the song out as not punk enough.

"A song like that is so vulnerable, and in a way, that's sort of what punk is," Armstrong counters, astutely today. "Instead of throwing your insecurities into a closet somewhere and keeping your guard up all the time, it's like celebrating it."

"Yes, it is actually a song that was finished during the writing sessions for *Dookie*, and we didn't put it on *Dookie* because it didn't fit," Cavallo says, confirming its vintage. "And we said, 'Well this doesn't really fit. We think it's a great song, but it doesn't really fit the album.' It took quite a while actually to figure out how to arrange that song and structure it. I played around with it for a couple of months before we went in the studio because I was like, 'Oh my god, I know this song's a hit, but we just have to figure out how to do it. How do we do this song?' And when it came time for *Nimrod*, Billie said, 'I think this song will finally fit.' Then I thought to myself, 'You know, the one thing that the song really needs is strings.' When I brought the idea to them, they said, 'Strings? Are you sure?' and I said, 'I think so. I think it's what the song really wants.' They said, 'Well, OK, we'll fuckin' try it then.' They were definitely open to it, but it was a risk."

Cavallo told the band to go play some foosball while he recorded the string section, and they happily obliged. "I don't know if they were uncomfortable or they were nervous, but they weren't in the room when the strings were recorded."

Ironically, the stylistic leap of faith was one of the easiest tracks to record and mix, thanks to its bare bones arrangement. "It took almost no time to get the strings done. We probably did it in like fifteen, twenty minutes, maybe a half an hour at the most. And I knew we had done the right thing. I knew it was a hit the second I heard it; I knew it was a hit. And I was so excited, but I was all casual and I walked outside to the other building where they were playing foosball. The window was open and I looked in and said, 'Hey guys, you just cut a number one single.' And they said, 'What?!' And I said, 'I'm telling you, this thing is fucking awesome. You're not gonna believe it.' I was really excited, so they listened to it and said, 'Oh my god, it's amazing.' They just thought it was amazing."

"Everyone knew it was a good song and knew that it was departure and knew it was nice to have on the record," Lord-Alge recalls. "But at the time they weren't thinking it would be [a hit]. You know, a punk band that does rock stuff isn't going to say, 'Well here's the big single for us, and it's a mellow song.' They're hoping that 'Hitching a Ride' or 'Nice Guys Finish Last' were the ones that were gonna make a difference."

"Hitchin' a Ride," a great track with a thumping bass line and an infectious "One, two, one, two, three, four," bridge, was indeed the first single off *Nimrod* and quickly became a radio hit, but nothing that would crossover or sustain the album on the charts (it would debut at Number 10). "Time of Your Life," despite the band's jitters, was selected as the second single.

"I was scared for that song to come out," Armstrong said in our interview for *Spin* in 2005, "and I was really excited at the same time. I thought it was a powerful song and it made me cry and all that, but there was just that fear of it coming out, and I never had that feeling of being afraid. But because it was such a vulnerable song, to put that song out and it was like which way will it end up going? It was really exciting and it kind of sparked more in us as songwriters to expand on that."

The song's presence and sheer reach across the culture seemed gigantic; from sporting events like Michael Jordan's final game with the Chicago Bulls to television dramas and comedies, it seemed to hit whatever note was necessary: wistful nostalgia, pathos. It was an all-purpose soundtrack to life's varied bitter sweetness. "We saw it take on a life of its own," Cavallo says. "We knew they were playing it at everybody's high school prom and all that kind of stuff. So yeah, we were very aware of it and we thought it was awesome. I actually think that adding the strings was key because it was sort of an early indication that you're not just gonna get one brand of punk rock music from Green Day; you're gonna get a lot of different kinds of music and it can all be great. And it can be something as heavy as 'Brain Stew' or something as fitted for pop radio and emotional as 'Time of Your Life.' "

"I was at a dentist's office," San Francisco disc jockey Steve Masters recalls, "and they were playing K-OIT, like the easy music station and that song came on. I go, 'My god, Green Day is on the K-OIT easy listening station. What is the world coming to?' They would hate to know that. I bet you they would hate that this program director, after Elton John's 'Candle in the Wind,' puts on Green Day. Oh my god."

Although *Nimrod* was hardly easy listening soft rock, reviews for the album (discounting acclaim for the single) were mixed—in the rock press at least. Green Day still seemed to be a band that was finding itself outside its punk rock identity. If *Insomniac* communicated "We still rock," then *Nimrod* seemed to convey: "But we can do more than just rock, you know. We are creatively ambitious."

"Anyone who ever griped that Green Day weren't really punk will find confirmation here," read a December 1997 *Spin* article. "At heart, *Nimrod* is a poker-faced rendition of what every band before them has done in this situation—genre hopping, 'testing their boundaries' in the studio, strings, horns, the works."

Still, the single kept Green Day from falling far off the grid, and pleasantly surprised those who were in the process of writing them off as scatological, arrested teens. "Can this really be the same band that helped reignite the punk scene several years ago?" *Billboard* mused in its November 29, 1997 edition.

Although "Time of Your Life" was featured in an episode of *ER* (nurse Gloria Reuben sings a soulful rendition of it at the funeral of a twelve-year-old boy) and the aforementioned Jordan retirement, the song is inextricably linked with the May 1998 series finale of *Seinfeld*. Played over a two-part package of clips from the groundbreaking sitcom's nine seasons, the track perfectly sets a reflective tone without the usually attendant sap.

"It has a nice ironic, yet elegiac, edge," *People*'s associate bureau chief and television critic Cynthia Wang notes, "which fits the producers' intention of a nonsentimental yet sentimental ending. It's not a far stretch to see how the punkish, outsider edge of Green Day matches a sitcom that was also unconventional in structure and topic. After all, Green Day covered masturbation in 'Longview' and *Seinfeld* did it in 'The Contest.'"

"I'm not really much of a TV watcher," Tre Cool shrugged at the time. Like The Police's "Every Breath You Take," it's ironically a dark and embittered song that's been widely misconstrued as a sincere piece of well-wishing: a love song. "If I'm going to write something poppy," Armstrong said of the song's complex nature, "it's got to mean something to me. If musically it's super catchy and almost sweet-sounding, then I've got to make it mean something."

"It's really about a girlfriend [Amanda] who he broke up with," Cavallo theorizes. "It's one of those classic stories where the song sounds like he's saying, 'I hope you had the time of your life and that you had this thing.' But really, it's not necessarily coming from a nice point of view. He's saying goodbye and good luck and good riddance."

The *Nimrod* promotional tour pushed off in the fall of 1997, and the band wasted no time proving that they had not gone soft. An in-store signing at Tower Records on Lower Broadway in Manhattan was scheduled around a Conan O'Brien appearance and a sold-out concert at the Roseland Ballroom. Stung by some reviews that suggested they'd gone a bit soft, Green Day woke up their dormant punk brat schtick once more. The trio turned an eight-song set into yet another riot, albeit a small one, contained behind storefront glass like a school science exhibit on punk attitude. While four hundred fans gathered inside and one thousand more lined the streets, shivering in the unseasonable chill, Billie Joe upended CD racks and tagged "Fuck" and "Nimrod" on the storefront windows in black spray paint. He mooned the people who were outside. When it was over, Cool tossed his bass drum into the throng.

No charges were filed and nobody was hurt, but Tower staff had to close the store down to repair the damages and clean up. When they opened in the morning, "Fuck" and "Nimrod" remained exposed until the windows could be replaced.

The incident brought them another blip of national attention, but this go-around something about it sparked of contrivance: the kind of "Give the people what we think they want" punk mentality that prevented acts like the Ramones, brilliant as they were, from altering their assault strategies over the years. Green Day had taken one remarkable step forward with "Good Riddance," and here they were backsliding in New York City. "If you look at their career," suggests Baltudis, who scrambled to rush-issue a post-riot press release that evening, "it *does* go in waves. There are waves of them recognizing certain [public] perceptions and waves of them [defying them]. I think the band felt pressure to live up to expectations that day. They were in the media capital of the world. We had press at the event. And so they made a statement. But the difference between Tower and Woodstock was that Tower appeared to be more calculated. And I think they did take a measurable amount of flack for it [from the media]. Like 'Oh, how obvious! Destroy fixtures in a record store. It's punk rock. Kinda.'"

That June, while playing K-ROQ's sixth annual "Weenie Roast" festival at Irvine Meadows Amphitheater, Dirnt was injured onstage again after an altercation with fellow Bay

Area hit makers Third Eye Blind. Third Eye bassist Arion Salazar, ostensibly drunk, rushed the stage during Green Day's set and bear-hugged his fellow bass-man. Dirnt shook him off and security manhandled Salazar into the wings. This irked a Third Eye Blind fan, who threw a bottle at Dirnt's head; he suffered a fractured skull and cuts.

"I am sorry that my attempt at doing something I thought would be funny escalated into Mike getting hurt. That was never my intention. I simply had too much to drink and made a very bad decision. If I had been in Mike's place, I'm sure I would have acted similarly. My heart goes out to him, and I hope he recovers quickly. We have many friends in common, and I just hope that they can accept my sincerest apology. I am sorry, Mike."

"On the advice of their attorneys, Green Day are unable to comment at this time," the band shrugged in an official response. "Stay tuned."

Happily, the *Nimrod* tour is most notable for the debut of a ritual that exists to this day at every Green Day tour stop: turning over their instruments to random members of the audience and standing back as fans take over the stage. "I saw them play in a show in London and then in Paris," says rock photographer Bob Gruen, who was out shooting the band as they toured Europe with openers D Generation. "And that's when they were first exchanging a guitar player, you know, getting somebody to come up out of the audience. It really just involves the whole audience so much. The fact that they pass some kid up. I saw them one time where they had the kid literally jump out of the balcony and get caught by the crowd and passed up through the audience toward the stage."

The nightly ritual usually begins about three quarters of the way into the set, with Armstrong asking who can play the drums (prompting the kids in the pit to swear that they can keep a minimal four on the floor beat). "Do you swear?" he pushes. A natural showman, Armstrong knows that the momentum can be killed at any moment if the bit (and the beat) falls flat. "Do you fucking swear? All right, get up here."

"The crowd surfed me up to the security guard, waiting at the end of the ramp," says twenty-two-year-old New Jersey fan Sarah Elizabeth Royal, who played guitar during the September 2005 Giants Stadium show. "Everyone around me is screaming. I'm all psyched up and the security guard tells me to relax. So I say 'OK' and cool down. He sits me up on the end of the stage, now I'm facing the kids in the front row. I pull myself up onstage, jog up the ramp, and see Billie Joe waiting there for me. He was holding his hands out as if to hug me. I gave him a hug. As soon as I let go, he grabbed my face on either side and pulled me toward him and planted a big kiss right on my lips. Then he kind of laughed, and I held my hands up in triumph."

The ad hoc band of fans always play "Knowledge" by Operation Ivy because it's a perfect nod to Green Day's populist roots and because it's really hard to screw up. Anticipating the stage nerves they've long since mastered, the first thing the band does is try to focus their new charges. " 'This is going to be real simple; you'll be OK. Three chords, OK?' " Royal continues: "Billie was definitely warm and wanted to make sure I was comfortable and wouldn't freak out. I knew the song by heart. I'd practiced it at home. But for half a second I freaked out in my mind because I thought he was playing something different. I ended up regaining my senses and nodded that I understood. He put the guitar on me and I hastily reached out for him to hand me a pick. I fretted. My hands were shaking terribly."

When the song is over and the nerves turn to pure adrenaline, the guitarist usually gets to keep the guitar he or she has played (the bassist and drummer are out of luck). One of the fans is encouraged to dive into the crowd (complete with drum roll and sometimes a mock cry of "Get the fuck off my stage!"). Maybe the fans will go on to form their own bands— that's the implicit gesture anyway, a passing of the torch, just as Operation Ivy passed it to Green Day in 1989.

"They play 'Knowledge' at almost every show for years and years all over the world so that's been really helpful to us and a nice thing," Jesse Michaels says today. "A big compliment and I appreciate it." At a time when their fortunes were dicey (the *Nimrod* tour played largely to 1,500- to 3,000-capacity venues), the instrument-exchange part of the set formed a solid and deathless bond between artist and fan, one that would help them survive the next four years.

Chapter Nine

UNCLE BILLIE

By the end of the decade, Green Day found themselves in an odd sort of limbo commercially. Their Gilman-era fans had turned thirty. Many of them had settled down. The club even lifted its ban on Green Day members, by booking Dirnt's side project The Frustrators for a gig. "For me, it was a wonderful piece of closure," Dirnt said in *Guitar World*'s September 2000 issue. "I didn't get one iota of shit from anyone there. 'Cause people know where we're coming from and that we're not full of shit."

The complete Green Day lineup would perform a stealth show for about a hundred truly shocked fans (almost none of them irate) in 2003. They took the stage unannounced before a set by Jason White's band the Influents, blew the door out, and then left: a nice bit of guerilla closure, nearly a decade after first being banned. Closure was a big deal at the end of the millennium. Unfortunately, this meant that a noticeable measure of the band's fan base was putting the cap on their own decade of adolescent angst.

The *Dookie*-era teenage fans were heading off to college and listening to indie rock or classic jazz (or whatever else impressed the opposite sex on campus). And the new generation of kids seemed, for the time being anyway, way too intoxicated by the one-click variety of file sharing, which had become (in its pre-iTunes/Napster period) an unsettling force that threatened to destabilize any and all lasting, loyal fan bases and make relics out of album buyers. Punk had ceded to ska, which flickered a bit, then quickly ceded to rap-metal. Korn, Limp Bizkit, and Kid Rock were the new modern rock superstars and radio formats changed accordingly. Three-chord pop-punk with no DJ to scratch on the explosive chorus seemed played out. Green Day could only sit and observe, somewhat bemusedly, maybe a little worried as the baseball cap alarmingly replaced the Mohawk.

Billie, Mike, and Tre had been together a decade now as Green Day. They had toured and recorded almost constantly in that time, and certainly earned a break. They all had other interests. Their children were walking and talking now. They were nearing thirty themselves. It was time to reconsider things. The millennium was ending and so, it seemed, was the manic phase of Green Day's career.

"They were definitely at a very big crossroads," recalls John Lucasey, a former Hollywood stuntman in big budget actioners like *The Rock*, turned owner of Oakland's Studio 880 (where Green Day's new album would be recorded).

The most symbolic indicator that this would be Green Day's new direction was the fact that they initially opted to work with a different producer. Rob Cavallo would take a back seat to sought-after modern rock helmer Scott Litt (whose credits included Nirvana and R.E.M.).

There was tension in the studio, however, as Green Day and Litt labored to come up with something that would signal the next phase of the band's career.

"It just didn't work out," Armstrong explained to the *Alternative Press*. "He was really cool, but for that particular project, it just wasn't the right chemistry."

In February it was announced that Litt was out and Cavallo

was back in, although in a limited capacity, as "executive producer." Green Day would otherwise handle it all on their own.

One album that hinted at the kind of statement the band was going for was Bob Dylan's *Bringing It All Back Home*. The 1964 release was half free-form electric blues, half acoustic folk rambles and protests. Armstrong listened to it over and over again during the writing and early recording sessions for what would become Green Day's sixth album, *Warning*.

"Billie mentioned in passing, 'I've been listening to a lot of old Bob Dylan lately, especially that album where he first used a band,'" Larry Livermore wrote in the Reprise bio that was sent out with the record. "I know the album. It is called *Bringing It All Back Home*, and I suddenly realized that this was what the new Green Day record was all about."

The year 2000, like 1964, was an election year. Bill Clinton was a lame duck and as his vice president, Al Gore campaigned against George W. Bush, the son of forty-first president George H. W. Bush.

"I don't know that he was thinking as politically as he would," Cavallo says, "but he *was* thinking more socially. It could have been a little bit of foreshadowing of things to come."

"*I want to be the minority,*" Armstrong sang on the chorus of what would be the new record's standout track, "Minority."

"*I don't need your authority. Down with the moral majority . . .*" As if a nod to Dylan, the song was propelled by a folky harmonica line.

It was Green Day's most overt political statement to date, something that may not have made the late Tim Yohannan reconsider his dismissal, but it was certainly not another "pot song" or a "girl song" or a "shit song."

"We've always tried to keep our ear to the ground and keep our eyes open to what's going on," Armstrong said in 2005. "We were starting to think about how there was going to be a changing of the guard from Clinton to somebody else. It didn't look good for Al Gore. It was just sort of a feeling that I knew there was going to be someone really conservative who was going to come into office. And after he was elected, we watched the culture sort of sway. And that's one reason why I was really taking my time writing songs to really [make an impact]. Instead of just writing an overly knee jerk reaction."

Once the record was near completion, the band announced to the surprise of many that they would join that summer's sixth annual Warped Tour. Warped had started as a small package tour for up-and-coming punk bands and extreme sports stars but had quickly evolved into one of the season's biggest live draws. Green Day were the obvious headliners, although Warped, much like Gilman, made a policy of not identifying any one artist as such. Although hardly a staunch boot camp for cred-Nazis, Warped was no easy gig either. Eminem had debuted there the previous year and was roundly booed. To play convincingly, Green Day had to reconnect with some measure of rawness that they'd left behind.

Warped was no haven for nu metal acts either. It was strictly guitars and three-chord, pogo-friendly punk rock, so synergizing was a keen career move, when to some, it may have looked like a downgrade.

"We'd been asked to play it before," Dirnt said. "But we never had the time. They've done a really good thing with that tour. It was just a good time for us to [finally] play it."

Their old friend Jason White, of Pinhead Gunpowder, was hired as a second guitarist to give their songs a bit more power for the festival circuit, but even he shared the sentiment that maybe Green Day were a bit beyond it all. "Even I was like 'Why are Green Day on the Warped tour,'" he laughs.

The explanation may be as simple as this: They were bored. More than what it might do for their careers, spending the summer out on the road with three or four dozen smaller bands was something to do. Armstrong, Dirnt, and Cool can be restless types, and too much down time is often a dangerous thing. The record was done but not out yet. Rather than waiting for a fall release (and making your friends and family nuts as you stress out over how this next change in direction would be received), why not play some parking lots and fields?

"They were the biggest band on that tour but it wasn't by far," Fat Mike of NOFX says. "Green Day weren't super popular at that time. I think they did the Warped tour because they *wanted* to get popular again. There's very few bands that can have a long career at such a high level. And *Warning* is probably their worse album, I think. It's what happens, the ups and downs."

When *Warning* was released in the fall of 2000, critics tended to agree with Fat Mike's assessment. Like all their records, it debuted high (Number 4) but fell out of the Top 20 almost immediately.

Even worse, the band were slapped with a plagiarism claim by unknown UK act The Other Garden, who alleged that the album's title track appropriated their 1997 recording "Never Got the Chance." Green Day denied the accusation and promised to defend themselves "vigorously," but the whole thing felt like insult to injury. (The suit was later dropped.)

K-ROQ played "Minority" as well as the album's title track and the gorgeous retro-pop lament "Waiting," but it seemed out of respect rather than genuine fervor. The station had largely switched over to a harder, rap-metal format.

"During that period, that was like late nineties, early 2000, they were kind of seen as elder statesmen," Kevin Weatherly says. "You had the whole rock-rap thing. And there was a period of time where we had a tough time getting that whole sound—it has nothing to do with Green Day—that sound we had a difficult time getting to work for us."

When Armstrong would spy any backward baseball hats in

the crowd at the promotional shows he'd play in support of the record, he'd shout: "Well, it's all about the dookie," mocking the title of Limp Bizkit's rap metal hit "Nookie." "We've been doing this for a long time, and we've had our ups and downs," Tre Cool observed philosophically. "If people want to buy our albums, that's great but [record sales] is not the kind of thing you worry about. Bands that do that tend to become jerks."

"It was kind of a strange time," says Jason White, who continued to play with them live through 2001. "I think more for the band than for music in general. It was the new millennium and everybody was kind of like wanting to forget about the nineties and wanting to embrace something new. By the end of the *Warning* tour, we were playing festivals in Europe and that was sort of when the Strokes were breaking really big. They were the new thing. And we were sort of still doing the Green Day thing, you know?"

It's one thing to be phased out by metal mooks or New York City hipsters, but to be upstaged by acolytes can be especially unnerving. In the space between *Nimrod* and *Warning*, Blink-182, a scatological pop-punk trio out of Southern California, hit the Top 10 with their blatant Green Day homage *Enema of the State*. Boasting formulaic hits (adenoidal verse, minimally pulsing bass, explosive three-chord guitar riffs tempered by sweet harmony on the chorus) like "All the Small Things" and "What's My Age Again," they quickly found favor with the new crop of teenage boys and girls (mostly girls) who now saw Green Day as a nineties thing.

"I don't mind Blink-182," Armstrong said diplomatically in 2000. "It's gonna be tough for them. They're gonna be judged by a couple of songs for a while. It just depends on what they come up with next. You can't judge a band by one record."

"Is this your older brother's pop punk band?" *Spin* asked in its review of *Warning*. "Have Blink-182 rendered them obsolete?" The magazine gave it a lukewarm 6 out of a possible 10.

Ironically, most of these younger bands, like Good Charlotte, whose 2001 release *Lifestyles of the Rich and Famous* also outsold *Warning*, hero-worshipped Green Day. These were the kids who purchased *Dookie* in junior high.

"They're probably my favorite band of all time," says Good Charlotte cofounder Joel Madden. "They opened me up to punk rock. We got into the Bay Area stuff like Rancid through them. Anything they said they liked in their interviews, we got into. We discovered the Clash through Green Day! I was definitely aware that our record at the time sold more maybe than their record but I think we idolized them so much that it didn't matter. We thought *Warning* was one of their best records." While the amount of respect paid by these bands was considerable, the mass audiences proved to be fickle.

In late 2001, Green Day shocked many older fans by announcing that they would be joining Blink on a co-headlining arena tour in the coming year. Dubbed "Pop Disaster," it would be a "shared bill" with the younger band headlining in certain markets and Green Day topping in others. Although they were far outselling Green Day at this point in their careers, the notion of Blink-182 headlining over Green Day was somewhat akin to Frank Sinatra Jr. headlining over Frank Sinatra.

"We really wanted to be part of an event," Armstrong told *USA Today* early in the new year, with typical honesty. "We figured putting the two biggest pop punk bands on the planet together was definitely going to be an event."

"A band like Blink-182 is nowhere near as genuine, original, or talented as Green Day," Gina Arnold wrote in the *Sonoma County Independent* that fall. "But when a band is surrounded by imitators, it's easy to lose sight of it in the crowd."

"Green Day have a strong economic model," Courtney Love theorizes, "and so people are going to come and flood the market. That's why they're one of those bands that have a million and one copycats. Lots of baby Green Days. There are lots of baby Nirvanas too. And they all kind of suck. If Nirvana had stuck around, with Kurt's level of ambition, which I personally know to have been vast, I think he would have seen some peaks and valleys as well, with his attitude and making *In Utero*. He would have had to get down to it and try."

Pop Disaster was all about trying, swallowing some pride, and reminding the old fans (and demonstrating for the new) who started this pop-punk thing (well, after the Dickies and the Descendents, anyway).

"Green Day were a huge influence for us when we very first started, for sure," ex–Blink-182 member Mark Hoppus says today. "And they definitely paved the way for punk bands being played on the radio, for punk bands getting signed to major labels, for punk bands getting exposure and just people being aware of that style of music, you know? It was with them that I think mainstream America started to take notice once again. It's all cyclical, you know? Through the history of punk rock, there have been bands that have really caught the attention of mainstream America. But you know, it goes in cycles, and for the early nineties it was definitely Green Day and Offspring that were instrumental in focusing mainstream America's attention on this style of music. I don't know how the tour came together. We just wanted to play with Green Day."

Rob Cavallo, still their A-and-R man and friend, agreed that launching the Pop Disaster tour was a good career move, if not a sustained ego boost.

"They knew that if you said 'Hey, punk band!' they were not necessarily the first group you thought of anymore," Cavallo admits. "But meanwhile, they knew they'd started it, and they were like, 'What the hell? This isn't right!' So the tour was actually a plan that we all came up with together. We knew that their live show is their strength. Basically the idea was to blow Blink-182 off the stage every night."

Green Day blew Blink-182 off the stage at every stop of the Pop Disaster tour. The band always wanted to be a perennial, like The Beatles, The Who, The Clash, the Ramones, and other legends they idolized. The threat of being relegated to a certain era along with the likes of Third Eye Blind lit a fire underneath them, and onstage, the band showed a hunger they hadn't demonstrated since touring with Bad Religion pre-*Dookie*. It was here that the pyro that would later be used to great effect on the *American Idiot* tour was first experimented with (Blink had no pyro, you see).

"I think it was a chance for them to relive their days of just being in a van," says Chris Cote of Pop Disaster support act Kut U Up. "I think it was a stressful time because it's a co-headlining tour; there's definitely egos between bands and they want to outdo each other. There's just pressures there. I think maybe it just brought out the fuck-it attitude."

Such an attitude would be vital in the coming months. In November 2001, after a contentious election with allegations of voter fraud, Al Gore, winner of the popular vote, conceded to George W. Bush, winner of the electoral vote. Bush, a born-again Christian, right-wing conservative, sent a collective shiver through the punk community, which had grown somewhat complacent in the relatively safe and prosperous Clinton era.

On September 11, 2001, the bands had just returned home from the successful Warped Tour, which found them flying all over the country, in some kind of extended, giddy state of regression. Watching those airplanes slam into the towers in New York City instantly erased any of those feelings.

"I think after September 11, I took a step back," Armstrong told *USA Today* three years later. "As an artist, you get kinda like hesitant, thinking, 'I don't want to speak too soon. I know something's going to come out of this, but right now I have to process things because it just seems so unreal.'"

However, as Bush led the country to war (first with the

Taliban in Afghanistan that fall in an effort to capture Osama Bin Laden, and then with Iraq, which seemed to many to have nothing to do with September 11 and didn't pose an immediate threat to the United States after being sanctioned and left in a weak state after the bombings of the first Gulf war), the band could only watch it all from home. You didn't have to be a paranoid Bay Area new radical to view it all as some kind of a premeditated ruse to secure oil supplies and line the pockets of Halliburton, vice president Dick Cheney's corporate interest. The members of Green Day were among those Americans shocked and outraged by the series of events. They knew they had the ear of millions of fans worldwide. Maybe less than before, but still enough to warrant some kind of statement. Others had been speaking out: Bruce Springsteen, Sheryl Crow. Armstrong, for a time, anyway, was not among the loudest of the dissenters. It wasn't apathy so much as it was a state of dumbstruck outrage. The band *did* post an anti-war petition on their official Web site, but otherwise seemed hesitant to revolt. This proved itself to be a common reaction among the generation of kids for whom he'd just spent the year playing. Armstrong monitored his CNN, like many Americans, and slowly filled up with anger to a point where something would boil over inside him, that could not be self-suppressed.

"Punks were still politically active under Clinton," says Aubin Paul, an editor at Punknews.org, a politically minded punk info hub. "But Bush has managed to slowly unify the left, which had been infighting for some time. A lot of bands who were relatively apolitical like Green Day were motivated by what they saw as an unconscionable situation. I'd say it went from a 5 to a 10 within a few short years. If you listen to the music released during the Reagan or Thatcher eras compared to the material released under Clinton, there is a bleakness and desperation there. Under Clinton, there were problems, certainly, but the sheer number of truly frightening issues under Bush had to wake people up."

"We all joked about when Bush got elected," Fat Mike laughs. "How it's gonna make punk rock good for four years." "The first time I ever heard Billie or Mike talking much about politics was long after *Dookie,* maybe around the late nineties, and even then it was more along the lines of general bitching about the government," Lawrence Livermore says. "The kind of thing you always hear in the Bay Area. I can only surmise that maybe as they grew older and gained stature in the public eye, they felt it was incumbent on them to take a greater role in the world at large."

On February 17, 2002, Billie Joe Armstrong turned thirty. The milestone was largely a happy one, celebrated with family and friends, although the kind of partying that the band were used to had slowed down a little over the years. "They matured," says Bob Gruen. "It wasn't all about just being drunk and seeing what party they could have that night. People in their thirties should grow up and by the time you're forty you should know how to live your life and not be getting drunk like a teenager every night. People think that to be in rock 'n' roll you have to be a teenager forever. And you don't. You can enjoy the rock 'n' roll, enjoy the music, and grow up. And have a family and have a life. I think you're more interesting if you do. You know, if you just stay nineteen forever, it doesn't look so good on a thirty-year-old, you know? But a loyal wife and a couple of loving kids does look very good on a thirty-year-old."

Still, what does a thirty-year-old punk have to say about life in suburbia? And with the war going on, isn't it a bit presumptuous to think that anyone would care? Always one to pour his feelings into a tune and then work it up so that it didn't feel leaden, Armstrong began his third decade by tentatively writing songs in a more reflective vein. The music and lyrics were slow to come. Frustrated, and wary that his creative block was causing domestic tension, he decamped to New York City alone. No band. No family.

"I went to New York for a little while," he relates today. "I told Adrienne 'If I don't do this, then I'm going to get really resentful. I just know I am, and you're going to resent me for being resentful. It's just going to be a double-edged sword.' And she said, 'Yeah, I know.' I think that's pretty much it. And she's been really understanding that I really need to do this." Armstrong, his hair bleached blonde, took very little with him: a leather jacket, a guitar. He rented a small apartment downtown and inserted himself in the East Village rock scene that surrounded bars like Niagra and Black and White and Hi-Fi. He spent his days, however, alone, walking, thinking about his life, the war, and his music.

"Being alone for me, I feel like it's a very safe environment," he said. "There's no one there to judge me or what I'm doing. It's just me, and that's when I get all my powerful stuff."

•

"When he went to New York, I didn't see him, but I knew some people he hung out with," says friend and filmmaker John Roecker. "Billie Joe is a walker. When he's pensive, he'll take these long walks. So he'd be on his cell phone and be walking, walking, walking, and he goes, 'OK, I'm in a really bad area.'"

"He said to me, 'Jesse, I'm a little blocked up writing wise, and I want to go to New York and get some inspiration and they set up a studio, a loft for me. And I'm gonna come in and write,'" Jesse Malin (co-owner of the Niagra bar) says. "We went out a few nights. The thing is that New York is an easy place in which not to be creative, to slack off, see people, and kinda get into a party mode. I know him and Ryan Adams hooked up and he ended up singing on Ryan's record. I thought, 'I gotta introduce these two guys.' They're both good friends of mine and great writers, and you know, they hit it off for a good while. And I don't know really what his full experience was but I know it didn't last too long here and suddenly I didn't hear from him for a while."

"A lot of people talk about that time and probably some of the ideas for what became songs for *American Idiot* were germinating during that period," says Gruen, who also hung out with Armstrong during this time. All-night, substance-fueled jam sessions were not uncommon in the makeshift studio of Hi-Fi's basement. "Ryan was drinking a lot," Gruen laughs. "I don't think Billie had really come to New York to be that drunk and so he went home. Ryan's got his ups and downs and I don't think it was the inspiration he was looking for. And so he went home within a couple weeks."

Armstrong took a bit of the sozzled New York sojourn back to the Bay Area with him. On the early morning of January 5, 2003, cops pulled his BMW over for speeding and administered a sobriety test. When he failed, he was arrested on DUI charges, briefly detained, then released on $1,200 bail.

Although Armstrong never made a big to-do about his fame and was described by police as "cooperative" he was recognized and, soon, the embarrassing affair was all over the new wires. It'd been a while since Green Day had enjoyed a hit single, and scandal, no matter how small, is no real substitute for staying in the public eye thanks to your work.

Chapter Ten

CAPTAIN UNDERPANTS

Green Day reconvened once again in Oakland in the summer of 2003 and struggled to finish album number seven, tentatively entitled *Cigarettes and Valentines*. The new songs were harder than the folkier *Warning* tracks: quick-tempoed punk rock that harkened back to *Kerplunk!* and *Insomniac.* "I feel like the last record is so complete that to try to take over where that one left off would be kind of futile," Dirnt said at the time. "We've had a nice break from making hard and fast music and it's made us want to do it again."

It had been more than two years since *Warning* and the stopgap release of *International Superhits!*, a best-of (featuring two new songs from the *Warning* era, "Pop Rocks and Coke" and the pop-punk workout "Maria," culled from unreleased tapes). Plans were made to issue the new record in the summer but once again, fate, in the form of tragedy, would intervene in their lives. Nobody will discuss just how the master tapes of *Cigarettes and Valentines* went missing. If you ask the band or their crew, there's a moment of "I can't talk about this" silence on the other end of the line. The vanishing master tapes for what would have been Green Day's complete seventh album are not only something they will not discuss, but also a subject that raises the dander of anyone associated with recorded music.

"It was not taken from here," studio owner John Lucasey stresses. "Everybody's fuckin' writing that it was taken from here. It was not. I mean they took their drives with them at the time. There was nothing that was ever stolen from here. There are safes, everything, you know? Surveillance, safes, I mean there's multiple steel doors that you would have to get through too and stuff."

Lucasey was, however, one of the few people outside the Green Day circle to actually hear the record before it disappeared. "I don't think a lot of people have ever heard it besides the band and maybe whoever took it," he laughs. "It was cool. It was a punk album, that's for sure. I think it was pretty hard-hitting stuff. Yeah. And that's about all I remember about it. It wasn't *American Idiot*."

The band had the funds to re-record the songs, of course. This was no new group with a limited recording budget. But the fact that they didn't says more about what was on the missing tapes than anything else, and unfortunately throws some harsh light on the ever-widening cracks that were emerging in what had once seemed like lifelong bonds. Armstrong had been frustrated with Dirnt and Cool's subtle criticisms of his work. The band had become a bit passive aggressive in dealing with one another. Rather than pick up from the start, maybe it would be easier to simply break up. Call it a career. After all, it didn't seem like anybody besides their most loyal fans would miss them. Armstrong would forge a solo career and finally live down the success of *Dookie* and the bratty image that seemed permanent. He could act his age.

They consulted, as they always did when business was troubling, with Cavallo, who asked them if they honestly felt that *Cigarettes and Valentines* was irreplaceable. Was it their best work? After searching themselves, they admitted that it was not. "I think part of them knew that maybe it wasn't when they called me," Cavallo says today.

It was decided by all that they would not act on anything just yet. The band and Cavallo convened and discussed their options. They decided that they were going to take another three months and continue writing. They also discussed the differences that had grown among them over the years. The small but unspoken moments of annoyance that can fester within any creative unit were flushed out. It was a Northern California–style "rap session," with Cavallo playing the role of the moderator. As New Age–flakey as it sounds, the results were liberating. The band left their Oakland studios the next day.

It was then that the masked "Europeans" moved in.

"The Network recorded here," Lucasey laughs. "They were in Studio B. Dude, all I know is that they had some crazy ass accents. The Network were really some fucked up, strange people."

Green Day are not the Network. The Network are not Green Day. That said, the advent of the anonymous, Euro-synth quintet (who are not Green Day) was the catalyst that allowed Green Day (who are not the Network) to get over themselves and eventually record the best music of their career. An amalgam of New Wave both great (Devo, Sparks, Kraftwerk) and terrible (every German band that isn't Kraftwerk), the Network, according to their official bio (released by Adeline Records, the label co-founded by Billie Joe Armstrong, who is *not* Fink, the Network's leader) are as follows:

Fink, the band's leader, who allegedly financed the album using money he made off the sale of a top-secret nuclear device. Van Gough, a Belgian who lost his nose during an Everest expedition. The Snoo, a former Mexican wrestler. Captain Underpants, a stuttering former Olympian. And Z, an Icelandic hitchhiker.

Money Money 20/20, released in the fall of 2003, features a cover of the Misfits' comic-core classic "Teenagers from Mars" and more lyrics about sex-starved robots than any other record released that year (or any year, with the possible exception of 1983). The record is a novelty, albeit one that genuinely rocks (even incognito, the Green Day quality control remains . . . coincidentally, of course). Even though they weren't, you could see how a band like Green Day, in their position, *could* be liberated by the sheer ridiculousness of it all, and the fun the Network (whoever they are) must have been having playing tracks like "Hungry Supermodels," "X-ray Hamburger," and "Transistors Gone Wild." Life during war time, possible crypto-fascists in the White House . . . a vacation in outer space is just the tonic.

The Network made their live debut at The Key Club on Sunset Boulevard in West Hollywood on November 22, 2003. The soldout event amounted to a New Wave dance party full of celebs (Vincent Gallo; members of No Doubt; and Trey Parker and Matt Stone, creators of *South Park*), sirens, lasers, and irony thicker than the smoke from the dry ice machine.

"There's lots of rumors about Green Day being the Network and it is preposterous," Armstrong, who happened to be in the crowd, cracked. "The only thing we have in common is we both want death to mediocrity in music today and we are all members of the Church of Lushology."

When interviewed at the venue, drummer The Snoo (who is not Tre Cool) would only say, "Sometimes, after band practice, the ringing in my ears tells me jokes. Fink is always complaining about Van Gough's mass cabbage consumption. He orders fifty-pound vats of sauerkraut flown in fresh from Bavaria every week."

According to Roecker (who "manages" the band), their Church of Lushology is like Scientology where they try to get celebs to join.

"The Church of Lushology. It's Billie and my Church

against Scientology. They're saying that we're in a toxic world. But our philosophy is that we should embrace that and put the toxins in our bodies so that we will be stronger. You know what I mean, so that we'll be able to survive. We're becoming one with the toxins. We're not being hypocritical about it. There's no dead alien souls. Just like, a lot of litter, maybe."

The Network (who opened a pair of club shows at the tail end of the *American Idiot* tour) are so enigmatic that there was a persistent Internet rumor (denied by the band sources) that the missing *Cigarettes and Valentines* was actually *Money Money 20/20*. It's seriously implausible that Green Day would follow a folk-punk release like *Warning* with tracks like "Joe Robot," but in a way, the Network and the errant *Cigarettes and Valentines* project are intertwined. Cavallo makes the correlation between something as ridiculous as *Money Money 20/20* begetting something as sublime as *American Idiot*.

"The Network was about finding a way into discovering who they were gonna be and what they were gonna do on *American Idiot*," he reasons. "There was a lot of artistic experimentation going on in the studio. And just the idea of like, 'Hey, we're gonna be somebody else. We're gonna press out and we're gonna do this opera and we're gonna be different,' was a freeing experience to them. And allowing themselves that freedom led them to sort of rediscover who they were and what they wanted to do, you know what I mean? It makes things a lot easier."

"Looking at it from the outside," Bill Schneider says, "they remembered how much fun what they do is. And it really just energized them. At that point for a band that hasn't had a record out in three years, they'd been in the studio for six months and now they had to start over and follow up a record like *Warning* that was not a great hit. Most people in that situation would be fucking scared shitless—their management would be quitting and their label would be wondering if it was all worth it—you look back and it all could have gone so wrong and they were so energized by it. But in the back of Billie's head, I'm sure he *was* scared to death."

Schneider adds, "Green Day are not the Network."

Chapter Eleven

AMERICAN IDIOT

As early as November of 1997, Green Day floated the idea of experimenting with a rock opera. A *Nimrod*-promoting profile in *CMJ,* seven years before the release of *American Idiot,* notes, "They began practicing in the same rehearsal space they've occupied for years, a garage rented from a more than understanding schoolteacher—and according to Armstrong, toyed with 'all kinds of wild ideas.' Maybe a punk rock opera. Possibly a two-CD concept album."

The back-burnered notion might never have come to the fore had it not been for a good-natured songwriting challenge instigated by Armstrong during one typically long and convoluted day in the studio during the trial new sessions. It wasn't designed to provide focus, it was simply a way to give Dirnt something to do while he was alone in the studio. On the day the "Homecoming" suite was written and the gateway to punk's first opera opened, Armstrong was set to register for his community service: the penalty for his DUI conviction. Cool, who was in the process of divorcing his second wife, Claudia (the mother of his second child, Frankito), had meetings with lawyers. Dirnt, who was always the first in the studio, the one who, in keeping with his upbringing, treated being a rock star most like a career, complained that he'd have to be there alone all day.

"Well why don't you write a song?" It was an acknowledged fact among the members that Armstrong wrote the bulk of the band's material. Dirnt was a songwriter but most Green Day songs began with Armstrong; so when he suggested it, Dirnt saw it as a challenge rather than something he might laugh off. "I decided to write this thirty-second vaudeville song," Dirnt says today, "and make it as grandiose as I could. Everyone came back to the studio later that day. Billie heard what I wrote and was like 'Oh, OK. This sounds great; I wanna do one.' So then he put one onto it, or connected his song to it, and he threw the ball to Tre, Tre connected one. And through the course of like a week, it ended up being like this ten-and-a-half-minute thing. And it kind of ended up getting this serious arc to it. It had all the energy and creativity and inspiration that something like either *Dookie* or *Nimrod* had for us. And so it was kind of obvious that this was something that we needed to be doing."

Dirnt's song is literally about being alone in the studio waiting for everyone to return. "I fell asleep while watching Spike TV . . ." it opens, quite inauspiciously. Armstrong's, similarly, concerns his own activity that day: registering for community service; Cool's concerns, in part, his divorce.

"I got a rock 'n' roll band, I've got a rock 'n' roll life. I got a rock 'n' roll girlfriend. And another ex-wife," he sings. It was absurd, sure, but for the first time in years, the band were amusing and inspiring one another. And the work, as basic as it was, was unimpeachably honest. More important, it felt physically good to write, to play, to sing this kind of stuff. After a decade as a mega-famous band, they'd relocated the freedom to screw around and have fun. "It's almost like what it was like to be alone in my room when I was rocking out in front of a mirror when I was younger," Armstrong said at the time. "I had a sense of freedom and abandon to take the record wherever it wanted to go. None of this was written from a perspective of like 'I gotta write smart music.' I look at all of our records as always having some sort of a progression, even until *Warning*. And [*American Idiot*] doesn't really match the progression of Green Day, really. It's got the energy of our early stuff, the dynamics and the way Tre plays. He's just a really reckless, insane drummer. And it's got all the power and the pushing hard, but it's definitely got something else. We've somehow broken the mold."

The band continued to build the suite over the course of the next week but still weren't sure of what they had. They were also working on songs like "Gimme Novocaine" and other less ornate bits that would make (or not make) the new album. They sent a tape of these down to Los Angeles for Cavallo to listen to. "Homecoming" was thrown on just to see what their longtime producer would think. Maybe he had a thirty-second song of his own to add.

"Cavallo called and he's losing his mind. He's like 'Dude I'm playing that thing over and over again in my office as loud as my stereo will go, and everyone in the fucking building is at my door going what the hell is that? That's the most amazing thing I've ever heard,'" Bill Schneider remembers. "And Billie and Mike were like 'Really? You *like* that?'"

"I was in L.A. and they sent that song down to me and they didn't really know what they had," Cavallo says. "They were like, 'What do you think of this?' You know, they were really curious. Is this great? What is this? And I played it and I called them up and I was freaking out. This is the greatest thing I've ever heard. I thought it was amazing. I loved it. The 'Homecoming' opera, that was a tipping point really. It was a song that broke the boundaries for punk rock."

"It unfolded after that," Armstrong says today. "We started talking about doing a rock opera. All we knew was that we wanted to tie it into the political atmosphere of what was going on. We had the song 'American Idiot' and it was better than all our other songs, which was great and frustrating at the same time."

"When Billie wrote 'American Idiot' it was like, 'Wow,

this far supersedes everything that we've been doing; this is the level we should be writing toward,'" Dirnt agrees. Armstrong was out blowing off some steam one afternoon, racing around the lot on a scooter that Go-ped had sent over for the band to toy around with when he had the idea for what would become the album's title track. He came back to the studio and began strumming out the riff and the one verse that had appeared in his head like a banner, waving:

Don't wanna be an American idiot . . .

The theme was not unlike that of "Minority," but it had a bit more conviction, a bit more urgency. It was a call and response. Like a gospel track or a hopping punk rock "oi" number. Something anyone could sing. "I Fought the Law." The "Limbo Rock." Harry Belafonte's "Day-O." The Violent Femmes' "American Music." The Mc5's "American Ruse." All were super-catchy touchstones. Any message couched in this bit of melody had to be righteous because it was the kind of delivery system that doesn't come around often. Armstrong thought of Bush, campaigning on a war ticket across the country. He thought of the man's message, which he considered to be a lie. The raising of the terror alert every time the administration was scrutinized. The using of the media to play him and his family and friends like puppets. The numbing effect of reality television and color-coded terror alert fear, which, he felt, turned us all into ostriches. And he spit . . .

"Welcome to a new kind of tension/All across the alien nation where everything isn't meant to be okay . . ."

"Minority" was a Clinton-era song. "American Idiot" was pure Bush 2.

He thought of the proposed constitutional ban on gay marriage . . .

Well maybe I'm the faggot America . . .

He thought of Pat Robertson praying for a Supreme Court judge who would repeal *Roe v. Wade* and institute intelligent design in schools . . .

I'm not a part of a redneck agenda . . .

Then he played the track for the band. "He got together with Mike and Tre and said, 'You know dudes we got to talk about something,'" Cavallo says. "'I'm kind of going out there with these lyrics,' and he played them the song once he'd done the vocals and they were like 'Yeah, fuck yeah.'"

"I think that since George Bush was elected, that we have led a path of destruction and mayhem and problems that are gonna stay with us and be with us for the next hundred years if we even go about changing them at all," Tre Cool says, adding with typical self-deprecating humor, "We're from Berkeley so we *have* to be political." When Cavallo heard it, the producer was floored once again.

"It sounded like the title track," Cavallo remembers. "Like a big important way to start a record. It kind of encompasses the meaning of the whole thing."

"I think that politically we didn't really have an agenda," Dirnt says. "The song just says that among all the different medias and in today's society right now with reality TV and all the media being swayed one direction or another and all the information being thrown at you and then throw this war on top of it, we've had enough and we're ready to say 'I feel confused and disenfranchised.' As individuals we feel like we're losing our individuality."

Still, in an age when anything vaguely suggesting a lack of patriotism had been enough to get an artist black-listed, throwing a spot on this common emotion, as sharp as it was, risked being wildly misconstrued. "This was a time in history when they were booing Bruce Springsteen for speaking out against the president," Jesse Malin says. "In *New Jersey.*"

"When they told me they were gonna call the record *American Idiot,* I was the one who was saying, 'Oh no, you can't.'" John Roecker laughs, "I was the one who was worried about it. Because when you think about, we know the song now, but then it was a really fucking bold thing to do. So many people got destroyed, like Sean Penn or Johnny Depp for saying one bad thing about it."

"We discussed the Dixie Chicks factor because it was reality," says Brian Bumbery, the band's new publicist at Warner Brothers. "I wasn't too concerned about it. I felt like a lot had changed in America even since then and that people were ready to hear artists take a personal stand through their music again." With the military casualties mounting even after President Bush landed on an aircraft carrier in a flight suit and addressed the troops under a tragically premature "Mission Accomplished" banner, Bumbery and those at the label correctly assumed the new material would now be something of a national catharsis rather than a source of knee-jerk outrage. Perhaps the Dixie Chicks did suffer so the likes of Green Day wouldn't have to. But there was still no guarantee. The Dixie Chicks were pilloried for commenting from a concert stage. "American Idiot" was loud, angry music. If it hit, it could have a genuine impact on the political climate. If it missed, there'd surely be more shrapnel.

Bolstered by his band's reaction to the song and Cavallo's enthusiasm over "Homecoming," Armstrong completed the second of the two pieces that make up the album's "rock opera." Armstrong had a rudimentary version of "Jesus of Suburbia" kicking around for a while.

"There's this Jesus of Suburbia character and he's pretty disenfranchised," Armstrong says, explaining the story line today. "He hates his town. Hates his family. Hates his friends. He needs to get out so he leaves and goes into the city. He starts dealing with what true rebellion means. Rebellion could be disguised as self-destruction. You get involved with drugs or self-mutilation. Or it could mean you end up following your own beliefs or ethics. He's sort of torn."

Saint Jimmy is "a charismatic scumbag," as described by Dirnt. "You know, girls want him, guys want to be him, sort of thing. Then there's Whatshername. She appears in the song 'She's a Rebel' and she's kind of this kindred spirit to Jesus of Suburbia. 'American Idiot' is the song that sets the political climate that our main characters live in. If it's kind of dark, it's just a direct reflection of the story being written in modern times."

"Jesus is the king of his local 7-Eleven," Armstrong elaborates. "And he's the guy who ends up leaving town. He's the guy who—he's trying to find out something more of life and he's trying to figure out what the truth is in life. And then there's the Saint Jimmy character, who's sort of the seductive, smart Darby Crash type of human being. He's the instigator. And then there's Whatshername, the person who the Jesus character ends up falling for. And sort of has—she's challenging, challenges his beliefs and his ethics so that's sort of where he's caught between two different worlds of Saint Jimmy or Whatshername."

As torn as Jesus of Suburbia is, our narrators were never more focused. Although they clearly had an affection for St. Jimmy, this was a process of intense creativity, not destruction. As they invented these characters, they were reinventing themselves as a new group, unencumbered by the past, but rather, able to use it again to write powerfully. Armstrong felt like Jesus of Suburbia. The punks he met in San Francisco as a teenager, surely there were many St. Jimmys among them. And Whatshername symbolized the nurturing female influence that was vital to his creativity from his mother to Maria Fiatarone to Adrienne. "I think I'm sort of digging up a lot of stuff in my psyche, like the whole 'Jesus of Suburbia thing,' which isn't necessarily about me, but I feel like I had to go through a similar experience to be able to write from that standpoint."

Nobody expected a band like Green Day to confront Bush and his cronies. They were arrested adolescents and had been for years. It was how we knew them. And in 2004, there was no reason to expect that anything would make them change. They did it so well. They were great knuckleheads.

"It's hard to go into new places just because you're so familiar with what you know," Armstrong says. "When you get into what you don't know, that's when things get scary . . . and exciting at the same time."

Imagine hearing the explanation of what the new record was about before hearing the music and you'll sympathize with the band's fans, both past and present, who read the Web-circulated rumors about Green Day's new direction in the summer of 2004.

"Green Day were done dude," says MTV's Gideon Yago. "I remember when people were saying, 'Yeah, Green Day's done this rock opera and it's anti-war.' I just kept wondering if they were serious. I was off the Green Day train, you know? I was a little suspicious."

"I saw Mike one night and he said, 'Hey Jess, we've got it. It's our best record yet,'" remembers Jesse Malin. "And god bless everybody, everybody usually says that. You know, Gene Simmons has been saying it for years: 'It's our best record since *Destroyer*.' Or Aerosmith . . . it's always that thing. And Mike said, it's an opera. And I said to myself, 'I don't know.'"

"Maybe people just didn't know they are smarter than they looked," says Chris Lord-Alge, who mixed the record. "When I first heard it I thought 'This is gonna fuck 'em good. This is gonna fix some wagons.'"

Fueled by how clearly he'd articulated his outrage (and how satisfying it was) Armstrong decided to juice up another song he was working on with some anti-Bush invective. "Holiday" had been a struggle. With a jumping bassline borrowed from

Iggy Pop's "The Passenger," the track had gone through several permutations before the band nailed it.

"I remember we went for sushi or something, we came back and then all of a sudden Billie was there playing it and man there it was, it was great," Cavallo says. "There'd been this big hole in the middle, during the breakdown and Billie said 'I've got this insane idea for the middle of the song, and it's freaking me out. I'm going to do something,' and he told everybody to leave the studio. And then literally, ten minutes later he called us back in and there was the 'Sieg Heil to the president gas man. Bombs away is the punishment . . .' He almost couldn't believe he was saying something so direct. He was not scared as much as he was thinking 'Can I get away with that?' "

Crucially, *American Idiot* is not pure anti-Bush rhetoric or bombastic rock opera. The album's humanistic core is key to selling both those elements. Two songs on *American Idiot,* both of which would become huge crossover hits, complete the emotional cycle Armstrong began with the songs "I Was There" and "Good Riddance (Time of Your Life)." Both "Boulevard of Broken Dreams" and "Wake Me Up When September Ends" have become part of universal pop culture now. They mean different things to different people. But for Armstrong, they can only recall Rodeo. Growing up, getting out, and looking back.

With the demos for *American Idiot* completed, the band headed down-state to Ocean Way studios in Los Angeles to record them. They all knew they had the best work of their careers.

"We showed up in L.A. and when they were recording it at the time, dude, I felt like I worked for the biggest band in the world," Bill Schneider says. "Nobody else knew it yet."

Slowly it was confirmed by the professional session musicians who came in to add their parts to what would be the band's most ornate production yet: a veritable opera with hammer bells, piano, horns, and tape loops. Multi-instrumentalist

Jason Freese, who plays saxophone on the "Homecoming" suite (and toured with the *American Idiot* band) had heard the rumors that the band were creating a punk opera. He had no idea what to expect when he drove to meet the band and hear the tapes. Would they be pretentious? Overly intense? He knew it was Green Day, but an "opera"? Freese braced himself.

"I showed up to Capitol Records [in Hollywood]," says Freese. "I walked in the room and I was really nervous. Tre comes down, there's this spiral staircase in the mixing room over there, he comes down, he runs up to me, and he goes, 'hey!' he goes, 'If you and I were camping and you woke up with my dick in your ass, would you tell anybody?' And I said, 'Uh, no.' And he goes, 'You wanna go camping?' Those were the first words out of his mouth to me."

With the tension broken, Freese, one of the first civilians outside of the band's inner circle, was played "Jesus of Suburbia" in its entirety. "It wasn't even mixed yet. And I just remember sitting there and just going, 'Jesus Christ!' I'd never heard anything like that in my life. I remember the first thing hitting my head was, 'This is either gonna be the biggest thing ever or it's gonna go over everybody's head.' You know what I mean? It was like, there was no middle ground. It wasn't like, this is just another pop song that's gonna go to radio. It was so unbelievable and moving and huge."

"I remember the first time I heard the demos," Jason White recalls. "I thought 'OK, this is insane. It's all over the place. There's nine-minute songs that are all these sort of little vignettes. It's kind of like 'A Quick One (While He's Away)' by The Who."

The title track to The Who's 1967 release predates their most famous rock opera, *Tommy,* by two years. The band's performance of the suites the following year during a guest appearance at the Rolling Stones' multi-act concert Rock 'N' Roll Circus was so incendiary, it allegedly scared the headliners into scrapping the project for three decades.

"Pete Townshend's definitely been inspiring for me," Armstrong says. "I've always been drawn to The Who and some of my first things I ever listened to was British Invasion kind of music. And I love his audacity, to take rock into that medium and still have that energy. That's where I want to go. I didn't want to get into writing overtures and undertures but there's definitely a couple of nods to Pete Townshend, for sure." Saint Jimmy is likely a nominal reference to Jimmy the Mod, from The Who's *Quadrophenia*.

Down in L.A., the band felt completely empowered. They'd indulge every creative notion that came across their discussion table. Longtime fans of her previous band Bikini Kill and her current, more danceable project, Le Tigre, the notion was floated that Kathleen Hanna should be invited to sing the album's recurring melodic section. The "Nobody likes you, everyone left you, they're all out without you, having fun . . ." line. A call was placed. "I was having dinner with my boyfriend and some of their people," Hanna says. "But it wasn't anybody who had any real connection to Green Day except my boyfriend, Adam, because he's in the Beastie Boys and he knows them. Somebody was talking about them recording a new album, and I said, 'I wanna be on their record.' I said something like that, this was like a month before. And then I got the call like a month later and I was asking him, 'Did you do something?' I was really pissed. I asked 'Did you call somebody?' And he said, 'No.' I asked Billie Joe and he said, 'No, we just were really big Bikini Kill fans and big Le Tigre fans and needed a girl to sing this part.' But isn't that weird? It was like I wished for it and it happened."

Hanna's vocal part was recorded in a New York studio then e-mailed to the band.

"Billie Joe was in the headset and he just gave me total direction. Like, no, do it more like this and it was kind of like trying to sing like a female Billie Joe."

Once the music was finished, everyone agreed that it called

for something different as far as packaging. Not just the album art, but an entire visual concept as well for the band members. Their live backdrop, their merchandise, everything should reflect the message: kind of like a political campaign. If Bush can do it, Green Day would as well. "We wanted to be firing on all cylinders," Armstrong says. "Everything from the aesthetic to the music to the look. Just everything."

"We were thinking of the concept for the designs [in the studio]," Roecker says. "We'd go to Wacko and the Soap Plant [galleries on Melrose Avenue] and look at these artists, and these like Chinese Communist photos." Artist Chris Bilheimer, who designed the *Nimrod* album and *International Superhits!* covers, was contacted in an effort to come up with a visual direction that would be at once uniform and powerful. Listening to the material on his computer, he seized on a line from the new track "She's a Rebel."

And she's holding on my heart like a hand grenade . . .

Inspired by graphic artist Saul Bass's poster for the Frank Sinatra–starring junkie film *The Man with the Golden Arm,* Bilheimer concocted an upstretched arm, clutching a blood-red, heart-shaped grenade. The logo that would follow them around the world, wave over every stage, and peer out from each CD sleeve jewel box was born.

"Red is the most overused color in graphic design. You know, Coca-Cola, Target, it's everywhere," Bilheimer says, "partially because it's one of the strongest and most eye-catching colors that's not horribly offensive like bright orange. It's so immediate. I'm sure there's psychological theories of it being the same color of blood and therefore has the power of life and death. And I'm sure there's psychological studies about it. And as a designer I always feel it's kind of a cop-out, and so I never used it before. But there was no way you couldn't use it on this cover."

Green Day, for all the teenybopper appeal of the *Dookie* era, had never been exactly sexy, and certainly, in their early thirties, the man-child crusty punk look they pretty much invented was no longer appropriate. The *American Idiot* campaign behooved something a bit more sophisticated. If George Bush was going to campaign in a suit, so were Green Day. Theirs would be black. Christian Dior, designed by rock fashion visionary Hedi Slimane.

"They were going to step it up," says Jason Freese. "They said, 'We're not gonna wear Hurley shirts onstage anymore. We're gonna wear suits. We're gonna wear nice suits too. We don't want to look like we're eighteen. We don't wanna look like every other punk band out there.'"

"Look at those early photos of Billie and his hair. He never touched his hair." Jim Baltudis marvels, "It wasn't a concern. None of this concerned anybody before. It was all about Billie's blue guitar and a little red tie. That's all they gave a shit about."

To fit into their suits (and the mold for what an older, wiser, classical rock 'n' roll star should be), the band went on a collective diet, ordering Zone box lunch delivery to the studio and their hotel rooms at the Chateau Marmont. "We were too cool for food," Tre Cool laughs.

By the time they met acclaimed director Samuel Bayer (who most famously helped with the iconic video for Nirvana's "Smells Like Teen Spirit" in 1991) to discuss the clip for the album's first single and title track, they all had lean jawlines, which brought to mind hunger and feral focus. They looked like fighters. They didn't want to appear too elder statesman–like, however. They still needed flamboyance. Rock stars are not like anyone else, after all, so they began wearing thick black eyeliner.

"Billie Joe really does wear more eyeliner than most drag queens now," New York City–based glam rocker and band friend DJ Miss Guys observes. "But they all had the face for it and could pull it off. I think it's great when somebody in the mainstream is doing something that's not just like everybody else. And punk boys look great with eyeliner and nail polish on."

They played the full record for Bayer during a pow wow in

the Marmont. "I was absolutely blown away," he says today. "They played me 'Jesus of Suburbia,' 'Holiday,' 'Boulevard of Broken Dreams,' and 'American Idiot.' Blown away. I thought, this is gonna be either the biggest thing that ever hit rock 'n' roll in the last number of years or people are gonna look at this record as a brilliant failure."

•

The band explained the album's story line as well as their political vision to Bayer and he saw, as one of the first people outside their circle, that they were all dead serious in their conviction.

"I understood very clearly from the band that, 'We want people to hear us and see us differently than they've seen us before.' You know, 'They're gonna hear a record that sounds different than anything else we've ever done.' I think my attitude was 'Fine, now let's make videos that don't look like anything else you've ever done. Let's make sure they're not just goofy and funny and silly. Cinematically, they've got a look, a style, and a feeling that's really provocative and really interesting and a departure.' I mean that's the key word here: Let's do something that's a departure for you guys."

"I'd be lying if I said there weren't skeptics," says Bumbery, who flew to New York City with five finished songs to play for the editors of various music magazines, as well as for tastemakers at MTV and radio. "But the music spoke volumes." Bumbery wisely included Green Day's online and print fanzine editors. "My goal was to take them immediately to the fan base they had amassed through their long and storied career and grow from there. I knew that word of mouth would quickly spread about how great the record was."

"American Idiot" hit pop culture like a lobbed, properly shaped grenade, muscling into playlists on pop, rock, and modern rock radio. Even if it had been an instrumental, it would have been huge, the riff was so instant. Many people hummed it without even listening to the lyrics. Bayer's video, featuring an upside down green and white flag, and the band in top shape, new look in full fly, laid immediate waste to every pop punk pretender going. It was like *Warning* never happened; it was almost as if *Dookie* hadn't either. That's how new this "nineties band" seemed.

Inevitably, the words "fuck," "redneck," and "faggot" (the latter being the song's boldest moment, perhaps, and certainly a show of solidarity with the Bay Area's gay community as much as a direct attack on the queer-bashing moral majority) were censored from mainstream radio. Still the fire in Armstrong's vocals alone made it clear that a powerful protest song, the likes of which pop culture hadn't heard since the heyday of Dylan and Lennon, had arrived.

"I wasn't surprised that they were gonna censor part of it," Armstrong says. "What was surprising to me was how some places were censoring the word 'redneck.' I thought that was kind of cool actually. Oh there was one radio station that won't play the song, and when asked why they won't play the song and they said because we have a 'redneck agenda.'"

Democratic presidential candidate senator John Kerry had, in most people's eyes, defeated President Bush in the debates, but in the weeks leading up to the election, he was once again trailing in the polls. Although Kerry's campaign songs skewed older, it was clear that "American Idiot," a genuine, bona fide, old school protest song, was a gift. Surely it was easier to embrace than rapper/producer P. Diddy's cryptic and vaguely threatening Vote or Die campaign. Had Kerry gotten on board a bit earlier, with "American Idiot" pumping at each campaign stop, who knows how many more eighteen-year-olds may have made the polls?

"We sat down and he insisted to me: 'I listen to rap music,'" remembers Gideon Yago of MTV. "It's important to listen to popular music and popular musicians because they tell you a little bit about what's going on in America.' And, after that he said, 'I think some of them might even make very good candidates. You know, they've got the charisma . . .'

Which I thought was astute. And then I said, 'Well can you give me an example? Who are we talking about here?' And the best he could come up with was Carole fuckin' King. I like handed him the fuckin' ball."

"You have to draw a distinction between the left as a whole and the Kerry campaign," says Aubin Paul of Punknews.org. "The Left could and did embrace the band, and the song, but the Kerry campaign seemed almost embarrassed by the youth of their supporters. Howard Dean rallied the youth while Kerry took it for granted and condescended to us."

Kerry and Green Day did finally cross paths when both were booked on *The Late Show with David Letterman* on September 22, 2004. Green Day had an album just in stores and had good reason to be there promoting it. John Kerry seemed to see an opportunity for some last bit of synergy.

"The Democratic party was so chicken shit with that election and the last two elections that they were afraid of really aligning themselves," Bill Schneider says. "And I'm sure that Letterman was a last-ditch effort. Kerry was not the guest. And all of a sudden all the other guests canceled and it's just 'Tonight John Kerry and Green Day.'" A source at the show, who preferred to speak off the record, counters: "We'd been trying to get Senator Kerry on the show for a while and there was finally some time in his schedule. We absolutely did not rearrange anything or cancel any other guests."

Kerry's backstage at Letterman photo op, much like Eminem's much-vaunted protest single "Mosh," released later in the fall, was too little too late to genuinely rally any voters. In the minutes leading up to the show taping, the band walked onstage and posed with Kerry as both their contingents watched with a measure of pride, but an equal measure of bewilderment.

"Kerry said 'I can't wait to hear that anti-Bush song,'" Jason White says. "I don't think he had heard it before himself. He was obviously pretty busy." The next day *American Idiot* would hit stores. The following week it would debut at Number 1 on the Billboard 200, a first for Green Day. One month after that Bush would win a second term in a mandate.

"We did our job. The youth vote percentage-wise was up more than any other vote," Fat Mike says. "But so was the homophobic Christian vote. They all came out too."

Defeat only seemed to rile the band even more as Green Day began their *American Idiot* tour in the spring of 2005, playing large theaters. "We didn't even know we were going to sell out theaters [when the tour was booked]," Jason Freese says. "A year later, we're selling out stadiums." On each tour stop, Armstrong's center-stage position would take on the role of pulpit. He'd demand the lights out for "Holiday's" "seig heil" section. He'd twist up his features like Bush and inform the crowd:

"My name is asshole!"
"My name is George W. Bush"
"This next song is a big fuck you to George W. Bush."

He'd introduce songs with instructions such as, "I want you to scream this next one so loud that every redneck in America hears you!"

The tour seemed, by its midpoint, to be a full-on anti-campaign, a youth rally designed to both entertain and enrage. "I think Bush's win definitely fueled everybody's spark," says White. "It was really disappointing. There's that glimmer of hope. I think everybody was sort of prepared to be disappointed but it was disappointing anyway. We sort of hit the ground running after that. This wasn't Toby Keith."

The band weren't campaigning for the Democrats so much as they were traveling America, while reinforcing American ideals and liberties, which seemed to many to be compromised with each new Bush pen-stroke.

"We didn't have an agenda," Mike Dirnt says today. "It's not a personal agenda anyway, it's more like 'I wanna think for myself.' That's all we're saying. [The record] is about raising a discussion . . . with really good rock 'n' roll."

True enough, Armstrong signed off most of the *American Idiot* sets by reminding his audience that they have the power to elect their own leaders.

"There's not one interview that you can find that really apologizes for anything that he says," John Roecker says. "Anything. You know, he just says the most insane things. He'll call me up, he goes, 'You have no idea what I just said.' I go, 'Oh my god, I cannot believe you just said that.' And I think people are really happy; it's refreshing because at least someone can be honest about it."

"If it was a concert in a red state," Schneider says, "Billie turned it on."

The *American Idiot* tour wasn't about amplified agit-prop, however. It was about bringing these new songs to the world. The band took care to play the new material faithfully to the note. "We rehearsed for three months before we even attempted to play it live," Jason White says. "It's almost like playing a Ramones set. No breaks. It's like shifting gears five times and playing five different punk rock songs," Mike Dirnt adds, referencing the seamless delivery of "Homecoming" and "Jesus of Suburbia's" various suites.

Armstrong, relying on a standard frontman's trick, would drop out his own vocals, only to hear them picked up by the crowd. At each stop, hearing their own lyrics sung back to them, often right on key and in time, seemed to provide the band with the energy they needed to mount such a production. Several songs, spanning their Warner Brothers career, were added to the set, kicking off, as their superstardom did back in 1994, with "Longview." Oddly, the Lookout Records–era material was ignored, but the fire the band brought to each venue (literally and figuratively as an almost decadent array of flash pots, concussion bombs, fireworks, and confetti were employed) was that of a hard-working,

Econoline-touring, and most important, still young and vital punk rock group.

"American Idiot," "Holiday," and "Boulevard of Broken Dreams" had all been major hit singles, and by the end of the summer, "Wake Me Up When September Ends" was issued as the album's fourth ("Jesus of Suburbia" would be its fifth and final single and music video). Bayer cast independent film actors Jamie Bell and Evan Rachel Wood as lovers whose lives are destroyed when he, an underprivileged high school kid, enlists for the sake of the financial and college benefits. As the band performs the song, combat set pieces are shot, showing the TRL viewers an idea of what may be befalling people their age in the Gulf.

"It's the one video that was really politicized, you know?" says Samuel Bayer (who directed clips for all of *American Idiot*'s singles). "I wanted kids to talk about the war, you know? And I didn't see MTV pushing kids to talk about it."

"It dared to show an authentic depiction of how the Iraq war costs young soldiers their limbs and lives," Michael Moore would later applaud in *Rolling Stone*. In January of 2005, *American Idiot* was certified double platinum (it would go on to sell five million copies in America) and nominated for Album and Record of the Year, the two top Grammy categories (it would win Best Rock Album).

Green Day first took punk rock into stadiums in England in the summer of 2005, selling out the 65,000-capacity National Bowl at Milton Keynes, a football stadium outside of London. "People were saying it's dead," Schneider says of the concert industry that year. "The Beastie Boys canceled their tour. Big bands like that were struggling. The band were worried. 'Are we gonna show up at Pac Bell Park and have people on the floor only, playing to 10,000 people in a stadium?'"

American stadium shows on both coasts, however, sold out well in advance, as did their two-night stand at the National Bowl at Milton Keynes, outside of London. These would be the biggest shows of the band's career, putting them in league (as far as box office goes, anyway) with the likes of the perennials: U2, the Stones, and McCartney.

"We were on tour with them when they announced their shows at the Milton Keynes," says Cyrus Bolooki of support act New Found Glory (who would along with Jimmy Eat World and My Chemical Romance open shows on the two-year-long world tour). "They only put one show on sale, and this was like on a Friday or something. And Monday they come up to us and, I mean Tre came up to me and he's like, 'Did you hear about what happened with our show?' I said, 'No.' He said, 'We sold almost fifty thousand tickets over the weekend.' And I'm like, 'Wow.' And just the look on his face and just like, it's the same exact way that any of us would act if that happened. Like the same way we acted when we found out we were going on tour with Green Day, actually."

"We played two nights," Armstrong remembered in our 2005 interview. "Sixty-five thousand people and it wasn't a festival it was just our show. We're playing these stadiums that are coming up in the States too. It's gigantic. But the great feeling about it is knowing that we're capable of playing [a venue] like that and that we belong there. It's not like we're insecure and trying to justify it. It's been like a seventeen-year career at this point and we're going into these places knowing that we've got these seventeen years backing us up, but we have something new and fresh to offer at the same time."

"British kids are probably the closest to American kids than any other in the world in every imaginable way," Imran Ahmed, a contributing editor at England's *New Musical Express* weekly, says, explaining *American Idiot*'s popularity in the land of Tony Blair, dismissed by the Left as Bush's cross-Atlantic lap dog. "The disillusionment and alienation in this country is so similar. The funny thing about this song is that it talks about America more like a British songwriter would talk about England. This America is really fucked up and shit. It has a 'redneck agenda,' you get called 'faggot.' This isn't the 'American dream' it's a fucking nightmare. And if you look at the great British punk bands Sex Pistols, Clash, that's what they did. They conveyed universal antiestablishment sentiment, usually about how shit Britain was really, in sub three-minute punk songs. I mean you could draw another parallel that Britain's fall from a position as world power throughout the seventies is being paralleled in the States today. But I leave that to someone else."

In March of 2005, Corey George, a nine-year-old fan from Wales, awakened from an auto accident–induced coma after his mother played him the *American Idiot* album for an hour, proving, perhaps in the most literal of all ways, what the band themselves had been proving for nearly two decades: Really good punk rock can indeed save one from a life of pain and suffering. It saved Green Day, and in turn, it saved their fans, both comatose and otherwise.

Through that winter and spring, award season for the entertainment industry, *American Idiot* was deservedly feted. It received seven Grammy Award nominations, including Album of the Year (they'd win Best Rock Album in 2005, and "Boulevard of Broken Dreams" would take the prestigious Record of the Year award the following February). Green Day swept the MTV Video Music Awards, the California Music Awards, and cleaned up at the Kids' Choice Awards (reinforcing their appeal at the playground, even as they headed toward the big 3-5). Even Spike TV seemed to reward Dirnt for the name-check in "Homecoming." At each ceremony, they put on suits, neatly applied their kohl, and graciously accepted the praise. It was as if they finally had nothing to prove, after a decade and a half. They looked like glam rock Buddhas at the podium. The once-conflicting sides of their communal personality were now finally coexisting.

"I think that way deep down inside, the truth is that Green Day didn't actually accept everything that happened to them with *Dookie* until *American Idiot*," Cavallo says. "I think they tried really hard and did a great job of it but the real coming of age and accepting of things happened here. They came full circle and grew the most comfortable in their own skin."

"When *Dookie* came out, Smashing Pumpkins were big and Billie would say 'Smashing Pumpkins suck. Billy Corgan, I hate him!' It was like *nobody* was good," says Anna Armstrong Humann. "And now, my brothers asked him, 'You ever meet those Fall Out Boy kids? And he says, 'Oh yeah, they're real sweet. They're real good.' He'll stop and say, 'Oh, I like them. We're a hell of a lot better.' But [this time] he'll be laughing. He likes everybody now. And he's really supportive of other bands. He's not slagging anymore. I guess he sees his role in the history of rock and realizes that he does have a place in it."

"I appreciate the success a little more than I did back then," Armstrong agrees. "I didn't know how to before."

•

"This level of fame has been very good to them," Courtney Love observes. "Billie Joe looks absolutely beautiful. You know how when people get super A-list, their face gets prettier? I think it's perception. It's something that happens in your subconscious. But he looks stunning. He looks like a beautiful girl."

"The Billie Joe Armstrong that I work with now is not the same guy that walked onto the *American Idiot* set a year ago," Samuel Bayer says. "Now he's a *rock star*. They were famous. They had done big stuff. But it's transcended that. But he hasn't changed. And they haven't changed. They're three friends who love one another."

"When I think of my friends, I think of Mike and Tre," Armstrong has said. "I look at Mike and Tre and I think that's a great couple of people I happen to be in a band with. Those guys are total fucking rock stars."

The critics and cred measurers will not go away, of course. They were there at Giants Stadium. They will be there when album number eight hits the stores. Cries of "Are they too young?" were no longer appropriate, but cries of "Are they too old" are inevitable. And "Are they punk?" will likely remain a constant even as the band continue to render the question personally irrelevant.

The punk fundamentalist cause was, for example, fueled in late 2005 when the band pulled their back catalog from Lookout Records after a dispute over royalties, prompting those old familiar cries of "Judas, dude!" "After a tremendously successful decade-and-a-half-long relationship with Lookout Records, Green Day is taking the reins of their Lookout albums, *1039/Smoothed-Out Slappy Hours* and *Kerplunk!* as well as their EPs *1000 Hours* and *Slappy*," a Lookout-released statement said. "There are no details as of yet as to what the band has planned for these great early releases . . . Green Day are an incredible force in music and Lookout Records is proud to have been their first home."

"All I have to say is, you know, it doesn't really affect me very much personally," says Lookout's Patrick Hynes. "Or in terms of like financially or anything like that. I'm not losing my job or anything like that. But it's disappointing. I kinda wish things could've turned out differently. I think that Lookout made some bad business decisions and they just kinda got caught with the consequences. So I think that Green Day is totally justified in doing what they did. But it still doesn't, it's like, eh . . ."

"I feel very bad about that whole business," Livermore says. "I do feel that Green Day didn't have much choice in the matter; they couldn't go on indefinitely putting up with not being paid, or at least I don't see any reason why they should have to. By not paying the bands on time, Lookout violated one of the most fundamental principles it has always operated by. It's hard to have sympathy about anything that happened as a result of that."

The world sufficiently conquered, and their indie masters back in their possession, for better or worse, Green Day are back in Oakland, playing poker and coping with what a source close to the band calls "post-partum depression." As of the summer 2006 they are building a new studio and plan to begin work on *American Idiot*'s follow-up in the coming months. There's also talk of a film version of the "Jesus of Suburbia/St. Jimmy/Whatsername" story line.

"I think there's been some talk about people wanting to turn it into a movie," Armstrong says. "I wouldn't mind seeing something like that happen. There's one journalist who mentioned that we were taking it to Broadway, and that just seemed really corny. We're going to Broadway! It would be *so* Off-Broadway."

"I'd like to see this thing done on ice," Mike Dirnt adds. "'*American Idiot* on Ice': Blood on the Ice."

Nobody knows what the new songs will sound like, but it's a good bet they won't be in the *American Idiot* mode. Even as they carry on without the burden of being "Green Day," the band will likely remain a creative unit that thrives on laying down challenges for themselves. Maybe the record will take them even further away from the three-chord, two-and-a-half-minute punk rock they started playing as teenagers? There's no need to resort to such things as a fallback anymore, after all. Either way, as long as a new Green Day song exists, punk rockers will go on, if only to loudly grumble about them. The band may still find themselves hurt by some of this. As Jello Biafra pointed out, they are human, and even if you're a high school dropout, there's a little bit of that eleventh-grade peer pressure terror in all of us. But being Green Day has ceased to become a choice since *American Idiot*. It's now, merely, a fact. Anything else, even punk rock, will always take a back seat.

"Well, you know, for me punk has always been about doing things your own way," Armstrong said in 2005. "What it represents for me is an ultimate freedom and sense of individuality. Which basically becomes a metaphor for life and the way you want to live it. So as far as Green Day is concerned, I really want the band to form into its own thing and not just try to represent all of what punk rock is, because you then alienate people and you also alienate yourself. It's about remaining passionate in punk rock but at the same time just really doing your own thing so its not just about writing punk rock music, but writing Green Day music."

And what's more punk rock than that, anyway? It's zen . . . or something. By disavowing punk, they become everpunker. And the genre moves on, preserved by the very forces that some criticize as a great threat to its survival.

"It's like in *Casablanca* at the end when Victor Lazlo is trying to get Humphrey Bogart to agree to let him out of the country," says Jesse Malin. "He says, 'With you on our side, I know we'll win. We'll fight against fascism.' That's how I feel. If we have Green Day on our side, we're alright. We got Henry Rollins too, and he's tough."

1039/Smoothed Out Slappy Hours (Lookout Records)
Release Date: April 19, 1991
Track list:

1. "At the Library"
2. "Don't Leave Me"
3. "I Was There"
4. "Disappearing Boy"
5. "Green Day"
6. "Going to Pasalacqua"
7. "16"
8. "Road to Acceptance"
9. "Rest"
10. "The Judge's Daughter"
11. "Paper Lanterns"
12. "Why Do You Want Him?"
13. "409 in Your Coffeemaker"
14. "Knowledge"
15. "1,000 Hours"
16. "Dry Ice"
17. "Only of You"

18. "The One That I Want"
19. "I Want to Be Alone"

Produced by Green Day

Kerplunk! (Lookout Records)
Release Date: January 17, 1992
Track List:

1. "2,000 Light Years Away"
2. "One for the Razorbacks"
3. "Welcome to Paradise"
4. "Christie Road"
5. "Private Ale"
6. "Dominated Love Slave"
7. "One of My Lies"
8. "80"
9. "Android"
10. "No One Knows"
11. "Who Wrote Holden Caulfield"
12. "Words I Might Have Ate"
13. "Sweet Children"
14. "Best Thing in Town"
15. "Strangeland"
16. "My Generation"

Produced by Green Day and John Kiffmeyer

Dookie (Reprise Records)
Release Date: February 1, 1994
Track List:

1. "Burnout"
2. "Having a Blast"
3. "Chump"
4. "Longview"

5. "Welcome to Paradise"
6. "Pulling Teeth"
7. "Basket Case"
8. "She"
9. "Sassafras Roots"
10. "When I Come Around"
11. "Coming Clean"
12. "Emenius Sleepus"
13. "In the End"
14. "F.O.D. (Fuck Off and Die)"
15. "All by Myself"

Produced by Green Day and Rob Cavallo

Insomniac (Reprise Records)
Release Date: October 10, 1995
Track List:

1. "Armatage Shanks"
2. "Brat"
3. "Stuck With Me"
4. "Geek Stink Breath"
5. "No Pride"
6. "Bab's Uvula Who?"
7. "86"
8. "Panic Song"
9. "Stuart and the Ave"
10. "Brain Stew"
11. "Jaded"
12. "Westbound Sign"
13. "Tight Wad Hill"
14. "Walking Contradiction"

Produced by Green Day and Rob Cavallo

Nimrod (Reprise Records)
Release Date: October 14, 1997
Track List

1. "Nice Guys Finish Last"
2. "Hitchin' a Ride"
3. "The Grouch"
4. "Redundant"
5. "Scattered"
6. "All the Time"
7. "Worry Rock"
8. "Platypus (I Hate You)"
9. "Uptight"
10. "Last Ride In (Instrumental)"
11. "Jinx"
12. "Haushinka"
13. "Walking Alone"
14. "Reject"
15. "Take Back"
16. "King for a Day"
17. "Good Riddance (Time of Your Life)"
18. "Prosthetic Head"

Produced by Rob Cavallo and Green Day

Warning (Adeline)
Release Date: October 3, 2000
Track List:

1. "Warning"
2. "Blood, Sex, and Booze"
3. "Church on Sunday"
4. "Fashion Victim"
5. "Castaway"
6. "Misery"
7. "Deadbeat Holiday"

8. "Hold On"
9. "Jackass"
10. "Waiting"
11. "Minority"
12. "Macy's Day Parade"

Produced by Green Day (Rob Cavallo, executive producer)

International Superhits! (compilation)
(Reprise Records)
Release Date: November 13, 2001
Track List:

1. "Maria (new)"
2. "Poprocks & Coke (new)"
3. "Longview"
4. "Welcome to Paradise"
5. "Basket Case"
6. "When I Come Around"
7. "She"
8. "JAR"
9. "Geek Stink Breath"
10. "Brain Stew"
11. "Jaded"
12. "Walking Contradiction"
13. "Stuck with Me"
14. "Hitchin' a Ride"
15. "Good Riddance (Time of Your Life)"
16. "Redundant"
17. "Nice Guys Finish Last"
18. "Minority"
19. "Warning"
20. "Waiting"
21. "Macy's Day Parade"

Produced by Rob Cavallo and Green Day

Shenanigans (B-sides and rarities)
(Reprise Records)
Release Date: July 2, 2002
Track List:

1. "Suffocate"
2. "Desensitized"
3. "You Lied"
4. "Outsider"
5. "Don't Wanna Fall in Love"
6. "Espionage (Instrumental)"
7. "I Wanna Be on TV"
8. "Scumbag"
9. "Tired of Waiting"
10. "Sick of Me"
11. "Rotting"
12. "Do Da Da"
13. "On the Wagon"
14. "Ha Ha You're Dead..."

American Idiot (Reprise Records)
Release Date: September 21, 2004
Track List:

1. "American Idiot"
2. "Jesus of Suburbia"
3. "Holiday"
4. "Boulevard of Broken Dreams"
5. "Are We the Waiting"
6. "St. Jimmy"
7. "Give Me Novacaine"
8. "She's a Rebel"
9. "Extraordinary Girl"
10. "Letterbomb"
11. "Wake Me Up When September Ends"

12. "Homecoming"
13. "Whatsername"

Other Compliations

1993 1000 Smoothed Out Slappy Hours (contains material from first two Lookout Records EPs)
1999 Singles Box (WEA International)
1999 Live Tracks, Vols. 1 & 2 (Import)
2000 Take 2 (WEA International)
2006 Collectors Box: Chrome Dreams, Foot in Mouth/Bowling Bowling Bowling Parking Parking (Wea International)

Singles/EPS

1988 Sweet Children, EP (Skene Records)
1989 1,000 Hours, EP (Lookout)
1990 Slappy, EP (Lookout)
1992 "Welcome to Paradise"/"Chump [live]"/"Emenius Sleepus" (Lookout)
1994 "Longview" (Reprise)
1995 "Geek Stink Breath" (Reprise)
1996 "Stuck with Me, Pt. 1" (Reprise)
1996 "Stuck with Me, Pt. 2" (Reprise)
1996 "Brain Stew" (Reprise)
1996 "Bowling Bowling Bowling Parking Parking [live]" (WEA International)
1998 "Foot in Mouth [live]" (Import only)
1998 "Hitchin' a Ride" (Reprise)
1998 "Good Riddance (Time of Your Life, Pt. 1)" (Reprise)
1998 "Redundant" (Reprise)
1999 "Nice Guys Finish Last" (WEA International)
2000 "Minority/Jackass" (Reprise)
2001 "Warning" (WEA International)

2001　"Tune in Tokyo [live]" (Reprise)

2002　"Waiting" (WEA International)

2004　"American Idiot" (Reprise)

2005　"Boulevard of Broken Dreams" (WEA International)

2005　"Holiday" (Reprise)

2005　"Wake Me Up When September Ends" (Reprise)

2006　"Jesus of Suburbia" (WEA International)

DVD & Videos

2001　*International Supervideos!* (Warner Bros.)

2005　*Bullet in a Bible* (Warner Bros.)

2007　Heart Like a Hand Grenade (directed by John Roecker)

ACKNOWLEDGMENTS

Thank you to Carrie Borzillo-Vrenna, my friend and coworker. Carrie did many of the original interviews used in the book, and did absolutely all of the driving in both Northern and Southern California. This book could not have been completed without her dedication and hard work. Thanks to Jaan Uhelszki, who did most of the archival interviews used for being here, another great friend and mentor.

Hal Horowitz, former lead singer of the Morning After, chose and coordinated all the great photos included here. Thank you to Hal and to the photographers, family members, and friends of Green Day who allowed us to reprint them.

Special thanks to James Fitzgerald and Anne Garrett of the James Fitzgerald Agency for all the moral support. Peternelle van Arsdale, who edited this book, for her vision, patience, and guidance throughout this long and sometimes bumpy process (and to Kiera Hepford, Miriam Wenger, and everyone else at Hyperion for all their hard work on the project). Elizabeth D. Goodman and Joni Mitchell (the hound) for putting up with my drama. Brian Bumbery for being a friend, and everyone at Warner Brothers Records for access to the press vaults (and the guest lists). David Townsend for being a wildly reliable and responsible transcriber. John Roecker, the cofounder of the Church of Lushology, for all the spiritual guidance and other things too. Pat Magnarella, Tyler Willingham, and everyone at Green Day's management for putting up with my occasionally stalker-like behavior. Sia Michel Dors Brod and everyone at *Spin*. All other journalists who've written about or interviewed Green Day over the years and provided source quotes or insight for this project (the ones I know and the ones I've never met). Mr. Brendan Mullen for being there for me yet again when I needed talking off the ledge (and some good punk-or-not-punk debating). Thank you: Tracey Pepper, Lyle Derek, and Chris Vrenna, Cheryl Jenets, and Melissa Sabella from Rob Cavallo's office, Steve Koepke, Marie Louise Fiatarone, Lawrence Livermore, Mark Kohr, Arica Paleno, and Anna Armstrong Humann. And finally thanks to Green Day themselves for being such an interesting and complex subject to research and write about, and for being a killer band. If you have to listen to one Bay Area modern rocker's output over and over again during the course of a year, you could do a lot worse . . . like Primus.

INDEX